# Understanding Educational Financing

## *A Manual for Developing Countries*

**Dr Jennifer Mohammed**

**Samuel Lochan**

*Published by*
Commonwealth Secretariat
Marlborough House
Pall Mall
London SW1Y 5HX
UK

*May be purchased from:*
Publications Unit
Commonwealth Secretariat
Telephone: +44 (0) 20 7747 6342
Facsimile: +44 (0) 20 7839 9081

ISBN: 0 85092 669 6

Price: £10.99

Designed and typeset by Wayzgoose
Printed by

# CONTENTS

# PREFACE

These modules on educational financing have evolved out of a series of seminars held in the small states of the Caribbean and the Pacific under the aegis of the Commonwealth Secretariat. Regional university communities, policy makers and planners from the various ministries of education and finance were the main participants. Their deliberations underscored:

- the vital need for personnel in both ministries to forge a deeper awareness of how each ministry conducts its business;

- the notion that workers in finance should be persuaded to empathise with an education project – a project that is deeply implicated in virtually all policies of national development;

- the portent of change in educational financing issues – trends toward decentralisation, school development and school improvement planning and, therefore, the need for initiatives that incorporate 'new' players, such as principals, senior teachers and community workers.

Insights from the seminars have been fashioned into these modules. They contain overviews of the issues to be explored, detailed content relevant to those themes, including definitions, teaching materials and extended interaction with the materials through boxed excerpts, reflective questions and hands-on activities, summaries, wrap-up stimulus in the form of a case for discussion and reference lists.

The modules can be used as a source of information by ministry, school and community personnel, as well as by researchers. A series of workshops could be planned around the specific themes contained in each module. The challenges and varied responses to educational financing issues occasioned by the inevitable worldwide changes being wrought in the institutional context of education, will demand that participants contextualise the materials, so making them more meaningful. In this way, the modules will be useful throughout the various small states of the Commonwealth and the developing world.

We hope that these modules will help in demystifying the jargon and ideologies that have tended to characterise educational financing in the past, and that they will promote greater understanding of its scope and relevance, particularly as it touches the lives of most citizens and institutions in every country.

**Jennifer Mohammed**
**Samuel Lochan**

# MODULE 1

# Development thinking and the implications for educational financing

This module consists of four sections which attempt to examine development thinking from the 1950s to the present day.

*Section 1* deals with human capital theory and modernisation theory in the 1950s and 1960s.

*Section 2* deals with the era of structural adjustment of the 1970s and 1980s.

*Section 3* deals with the evolution of the human development paradigm in the 1990s.

*Section 4* deals with globalisation and the new informational economy.

Each section gives some stimulus materials to be read, some questions for discussion, background information and summary points to facilitate understanding. At the end of the four sections there is a list of suggested further reading.


## SECTION 1

At the end of this section participants should be able to:

1. Explain the fundamentals of 'human capital theory' and 'modernisation theory';

2. Use 'dependency theory' to critique 'human capital theory' and 'modernisation theory';

3. Relate patterns of educational financing in the 1950s and 1960s to 'human capital theory'.

### Background

In the late 1950s and 1960s colonial empires were being dismantled and many countries across the Caribbean, Africa and other parts of the globe received constitutional independence. It was a time when Keynesian economics, aided by socialist ideology and the rise of the welfare state, created an outlook that fostered a drive to rapid growth and development. Newly elected governments were also keen to demonstrate the benefits of independence to their electorates. A theoretical justification was also offered.

## Instruction 1

Read Box 1. This excerpt is taken from the Draft Plan for Education in Trinidad and Tobago, 1968–83, which was drawn up with advice from UNESCO.

### Box 1

It is not necessary to argue the relevance of education to economic development but it would be necessary to indicate that we have passed the point of argument. Dr Adiscshiah, Deputy Director General of UNESCO and an economist, speaking in India in December 1966 said:

*But the function of education in national development in the considered view of a growing number of economists, and I happen to be one of them, does not end with the contribution it makes to a nation's labour skills. Its role is even more crucial and decisive. There is indeed a striking concordance between the amount of national income which a country invests in its educational system, and the rate at which that national income grows. In countries as far apart and diverse as Sweden and Japan, Germany and Mexico, the USSR and Israel, Czechoslovakia and Ghana, there seems to be more than an accidental or coincidental force at work linking high rates of educational investment and high rates of national income growth. Equally, a low rate of educational investment, such as is prevalent in India, Brazil, Greece, Ethiopia, Syria and Pakistan, for example, seems to be accompanied by a low rate of national income growth. Thus, there is a strong historical presumption that the key to growth is the rate at which the educational investment of a country progresses or regresses.*

Trinidad and Tobago must continue to make the investment needed in education or face the difficulties consequent upon failure. The Plan seeks to ensure that what is invested is efficiently spent. (Draft Education Plan for Trinidad & Tobago, 1968–1983, p. 6)

## Activity 1

1. What is the connection being made between investment in education and economic growth?

2. Is it right to assume that the relationship between educational expenditure and economic growth operates in the same way in both developed and developing countries?

3. In the 1960s and today, has it sometimes been assumed that in order to develop, poorer countries simply have to follow the strategies of the developed countries?

*Remember that the developing countries of the world sometimes have production structures that are externally dependent and they may depend on single commodities with unstable prices.*

## Instruction 2

Study the Table in Box 2.

## Box 2

### Table1.1. Educational Enrolments in Less-Developed Countries Combined: 1950, 1960 and 1966

| Educational enrolments | 1950 1000s | 1960 1000s | Increase 1950–1960 | | 1966 1000s | Increase 1950–1960 | |
|---|---|---|---|---|---|---|---|
| | | | Total increase % | Average annual rate of increase % | | Total increase % | Average annual rate of increase % |
| *Total*, all less-developed countries | | | | | | | |
| 1. All three levels | 79,444 | 146,567 | 84.5 | 6.3 | 218,381 | 49.0 | 6.9 |
| 2. First level | 70,262 | 125,502 | 78.6 | 6.0 | 180,040 | 43.5 | 6.2 |
| 3. Second level | 8,108 | 18,638 | 129.9 | 8.7 | 33,774 | 81.2 | 10.4 |
| 4. Third level | 1,074 | 2,427 | 126.0 | 8.5 | 4,567 | 88.17 | 11.1 |

*Source: UNESCO Statistical Yearbook, 1968*

## Box 3

The **national economies in the countries of "early growth"** succeeded in part because they were consolidated at the same time as the world market expanded, so that these countries came to occupy the leading positions in the system of international domination. From this scheme it is evident that "early development," although a very broad and imprecise term, is significantly different from what has occurred in Latin America.

It has been assumed that the peripheral countries would have to repeat the evolution of the economies of the central countries in order to achieve development. But it is clear that from its beginning the capitalist process implied an unequal relation between the central and the peripheral economies. Many "underdeveloped" economies – for example, those of Latin America – were incorporated into the capitalist system as colonies and later as national states, and they have stayed in the capitalist system throughout their history. They remain, however, peripheral economies with particular historical paths when compared with central capitalist economies.

Cardosa and Faletto *Dependency and Development in Latin America* (University of California Press, 1979) p. 23

## Activity 3

1. *What is meant by central and peripheral economies?*

2. *How do peripheral economies differ from central economies?*

3. *Does your country display characteristics of a peripheral economy?*

## Summary

Key points to consider:

1. Modernisation theory refers to a school of thought permeating economics, sociology, and social psychology which promoted the idea that developing countries simply have to copy the strategies of the developed. The newly developing countries simply had to follow the path of development which the more developed had followed. The richer countries were assumed to have 'arrived'.

2. Human Capital theory is part of the family of modernisation theory. In the 1960s, an economist by the name of Theodore Schultz produced research which showed strong positive correlation between educational expenditure and economic development. He argued that education does not only improve the individual choices open to individuals, but that an educated population provides the type of labour force necessary for industrial development and economic growth. Many developing countries have come to understand that the benefits of educational expansion can be very elusive. Firstly, the actual content and delivery of educational programmes have to be appropriate to culture, context and history. This is not easily achieved. Also education does not by itself remove structural features of underdevelopment.

3. The quotation by Cardoso and Faletto in Box 3 is representative of the Dependency School which argues for an understanding of the unique characteristics of developing countries as a prerequisite for any development strategy. Dependency theorists emphasised that the richer countries were undeveloped at one time but they were never 'under' developed. The colonial experience of a lot of poor countries left legacies of economic structure – foreign tastes, monocrop, dependence on imports, export dependence, dependence on foreign capital, enterprise and technology – all of which prove very difficult to dismantle.

# SECTION 2

At the end of this section participants should be able to:

1. Explain the meaning of structural adjustment;
2. Identify the philosophy behind structural adjustment policies;
3. Identify the effects of structural adjustment policies on educational financing in Caribbean countries.

## Background

In the 1970s, due to the oil price shocks, a large number of developing countries experienced crisis in their economies. The IMF (International Monetary Fund) and World Bank lent countries money under strict conditionalities. These conditionalities enforced a type of adjustment and a speed of adjustment which experience has shown as ill-conceived, if not highly unfair. The effect on educational financing during this period has been highly destructive.

### Instruction 4

Read Boxes 4 and 5.

---

**Box 4**

The main argument of the typical IMF/World Bank structural adjustment package rests on the belief that if governments reduce their intervention in the economy, and decisions are left to market forces, all things will eventually fall into place and there will be no internal or external disequilibria. The movement of resources to their best uses will optimise social welfare. A conviction that the market is the best guide to decision making and all human beings have the same materialist values and react the same way in all societies are common assumptions in all structural adjustment programmes, regardless of where they are being implemented.

From an article by Ramesh Ramsaran in *Structural Adjustment Education*, ed. John La Guerre, 1994, p. 20

---

**Box 5**

A structural adjustment programme is a type of policy reform which is espoused by multilateral international organisations, such as the International Monetary Fund, the World Bank, its affiliates and the donor community. Structural adjustment may be defined as a complex set of multilevel organisational and interorganisational interventions with multiple goals and objectives, a wide range of public and private sector organisations and organisational actors, with many intended and unintended consequences.

From articles by Khan Jamal, *Structural Adjustment Education*, ed. John La Guerre, p. 88

**Activity 4**

1. *What kind of economic ideologies are at the root of the IMF and World Bank policies?*

2. *Give examples of the wide ranging effect of these policies for any country with which you are familiar.*

*Instruction 5*

Read Box 6.

**Box 6**

A major part of adjustment programmes involves the mounting of wide-ranging reforms aimed at bringing about improvements in the performance and task orientation of public organisations. Well-known reform strategies include streamlining and improving public sector management, partial or complete divestment, liquidation or closure of public enterprises, decentralisation, and strengthening of the private sector.

Jamal Khan, p. 89, *op. cit.*

IMF conditionalities always attempted to level the playing field both nationally and internationally. All restrictions on foreign trade were removed. All government market interventions internally were resisted. Competition, accountability and self support were the yardsticks by which all organisations had to live. The mix of policies used across the globe by the World Bank and the IMF included:

- currency devaluation
- reduced public expenditures
- reduced subsidies, especially to consumers
- reduction or elimination of price controls
- revised trade policies intended to encourage exports
- revised fiscal, especially tax, policies intended to increase government revenue
- new or increased user charges for public services
- privatisation of both enterprises and social services
- institutional reforms required to implement these policies

### Instruction 6

Read Boxes 7 and 8.

### Box 7

The marked decline in the quality of education, and the grave implications for human resource development began to emerge in the late 1970s and accelerated in the 1980s. The nexus of high student attrition, absenteeism and grade repetition have resulted in low overall completion rates. The trend since 1982 reveals that a large percentage of students who finish Grade 6, possibly as many as 50 per cent, may be considered functionally illiterate, insofar as they read simple texts with extreme difficulty. A particularly disturbing aspect of student attrition revealed by the Survey of Living Conditions is the fact that 10 more boys than girls dropped out of school by the time they had reached 19 years of age. It was found that two thirds of the drop outs at primary level are boys, and half of the males who leave school do so in the first half of secondary school, while only 45 per cent of females leave so early. This phenomenon was described as 'highly unusual compared to most other countries in the world.'

Kari Polanyi Levitt, *The Origins and Consequences of Jamaica's Debt Crisis*, 1991, p. 53. Consortium Graduate School of Social Sciences

## Box 8

Even if the required government reduction in public spending on education, as well as on other public goods, was ultimately not successful, we argue that the adjustment process itself produced a negative effect on the shape and quality of Costa Rica's public education, at least at the secondary level. The attempt to hold down salaries and teachers' reaction had important negative implications for education expansion at the secondary level and special consequences for the distribution of education in the Costa Rican population. Access to higher levels of schooling for lower socio-economic class children became more restricted and different than in the past, and the general tenor of Costa Rica's human resource development changed. The policies also evoked a highly negative response in the form of lower teacher and parent morale. Therefore, the end result of the decisions made by successive governments was that costs of education were only somewhat contained but that secondary school enrolment and quality, closely associated with the democratisation of Costa Rican education, also never recovered from the impact of the crisis a decade earlier.

Martin Carnoy and Carlos A Torres in *Coping with Crisis, Austerity Adjustment and Human Resources*, ed. Joel Samoff. Cassell, 1994, p. 65 (UNESCO)

## Activity 6

1. *What was the effect on education of the IMF and World Bank policies in Jamaica and Costa Rica?*

2. *How was educational financing in your country affected during this period?*

## Summary

In general, post 1970 IMF and World Bank policies were frequently ill-conceived and when imposed led to cuts in educational expenditure.

Tilak (1997) makes some observations.[1]

1. Firstly, *the quality of education gets traded off for quantitative expansions* i.e. cuts made in staffing and materials while provision might increase.

2. *Equity is traded off for quantity.* School places might increase but less specific provisions for the poor.

3. *Mainly middle and upper-income groups benefit,* even at the expense of the sector relating to mass education. Investment priorities generally shift from primary education, adult education and other mass education programmes to higher education. The elites benefit from such a shift.

[1]Tilak, J B G, 'The effects of adjustment on education: A review of the Asian experience', *Prospects*, Vol. XXVII, No.1, March 1997, pp. 85–107.

# SECTION 3

At the end of this section participants should be able to:

1. Trace the evolution of the Human Development Paradigm;

2. Explain the main pillars of this new paradigm;

3. Assess the implications for educational financing of the Human Development Paradigm.

## Background

During the 1990s the commitment to human development has been made specific – and linked to time bound targets – in the declaration and plans of action adopted in major global conferences on:

| | |
|---|---|
| Children | 1990 |
| Education for all | 1990 |
| Environment and sustainable development | 1992 |
| Human rights | 1993 |
| Population and development | 1994 |
| Social development | 1995 |
| Human settlements | 1996 |
| Food security | 1996 |

In addition, 1987–1997 was declared the Decade for the Development of Culture by the United Nations and the decade 1997–2007 has been declared the Decade for the Eradication of Poverty. The United Nations Development Programme has begun to publish an annual Human Development Report which ranks countries of the world according to a human development index. This index factors in items such as health, education, transport, housing and political freedoms to complement the traditional economic indicators.

### Activity 7

1. From this brief list given immediately above, what concerns seem dominant in the 1990s and beyond?

2. How do these concerns compare with the 1960s and late 1970s and 1980s?

Read Box 9.

## Box 9

According to one view, development is a process of economic growth, a rapid and sustained expansion of production, productivity and income per head (sometimes qualified by insistence on a wide spread of the benefits of this growth). According to the other, espoused by UNDP's annual Human Development Report and by many distinguished economists, development is seen as a process that enhances the effective freedom of the people involved to pursue whatever they have reason to value. This view of human development (in contrast to narrowly economic development) is a culturally conditioned view of economic and social progress. Poverty, in this view, implies not only lack of essential goods and services, but also lack of opportunities to choose a fuller, more satisfying, more valuable and valued existence. The choice can also be for a different style of development, a different path, based on different values from those of the highest income countries. The recent spread of democratic institutions, of market choices, of participatory management of firms, has enabled individuals and groups of different cultures to choose for themselves.

*Our Creative Diversity*, UNESCO 1995. Report of the World Commission on Culture and Development, p. 22

## Activity 8

1. *How does the view of development advocated by the Human Development Report differ from that of earlier economists?*

## Instruction 8

Read Box 10

---

**Box 10**

On some aspects of the Human Development Paradigm, there is fairly broad agreement.

- Development must position people at the centre of its concerns.
- The purpose of development is to augment all human choices, not just income.
- The Human Development Paradigm is concerned both with building up human capabilities fully (through an enabling framework for growth and employment).
- Human development has four essential pillars: equity, sustainability, productivity and empowerment. It regards economic growth as essential but emphasises the need to pay attention to its quality and distribution, analyses at length its link with human lives and questions its long-term sustainability.
- The Human Development Paradigm defines the ends of development and analyses sensible options for achieving them.

Mabbub-ul Haq, *Reflections on Human Development*. Oxford University Press, 1995, p. 21

---

**Activity 9**

*Explain the four pillars of the Human Development Paradigm.*

---

## Instruction 9

Read Box 11.

*Points to consider:*
With gender, environment, poverty reduction and culture squarely on the agenda, education must aim at inclusion of all groups and include learning from cradle to grave as well as encourage participation from all stakeholders. This will definitely have implications for the quality and spread of educational financing.

**Box 11**

**PRINCIPAL ELEMENTS OF THE FRAMEWORK FOR ACTION**

**Goals and Targets**

Countries may wish to set their own targets for the 1990s in terms of the following proposed dimensions:

1. Expansion of early childhood care and developmental activities – including family and community intervention – especially for poor, disadvantaged and disabled children.

2. Universal access to, and completion of, primary education (or whatever higher level of education is considered "basic") by the year 2000.

3. Improvement in learning achievement such that a given percentage of an appropriate age cohort (for instance, 80 per cent of 14-year olds) attains or surpasses a defined level of necessary learning achievement.

4. Reduction in the adult illiteracy rate (the appropriate age group to be determined in each country) to, for instance, one-half its 1990 level by the year 2000, with sufficient emphasis on female literacy to significantly reduce the current disparity between male and female illiteracy rates.

5. Expansion of basic education and training in other essential skills required by youths and adults, with programme effectiveness assessed in terms of behavioural changes and impact on health, employment, and productivity.

6. Increased acquisition by individuals and families of the knowledge, skills and values required for better living and sound, sustainable development through all educational channels (including mass media and other forms of modern and traditional communication) and social action, with effectiveness assessed in terms of behavioural change.

Errol Miller, *Education for All: Caribbean Perspectives and Imperatives*. IADB, Washington DC, 1992, p.11

# SECTION 4

At the end of this section participants should be able to:

1. Describe the concept of globalisation and demonstrate the effects of globalisation on developing countries;

2. Explain the impact of information technology on production, trade and commerce;

3. Assess the implications for educational financing of globalisation and the new informational economy.

## Background

Over the last two decades, under the influence of the IMF and World Bank, free market economic policies have been the dominant paradigm. The removal of trade barriers across national boundaries has been a top priority of the IMF and World Bank. This has meant that local producers in any environment must be equipped to face foreign competition and to compete in foreign markets.

This trend to globalisation has been intensified by some other changes in technology which have impacted powerfully on production and trade.

Manuel Castello (1993) describes the emerging world economy as an 'informational economy' and defines four key characteristics.

1. The first feature of this economy is that 'sources of productivity and economic growth are increasingly dependent upon the application of science and technology, as well as upon the quality of information and management, in the process of production, consumption, distribution and trade', p. 15.

2. The second feature of the new world economy is the shift from material production to information processing activities.

3. The third feature is the shift from standardised mass production to flexible customised production and from vertically integrated large scale organisations to vertical disintegration and horizontal networks between economic units.

4. Finally, these economic and organisational transformations in the world economy take place simultaneously with the revolution in information technologies (micro electronics, information and telecommunications) around which a constellation of major scientific discoveries and applications (in biotechnology, new materials, lasers, renewable energy, etc.) is transforming the material basis of our world in fewer than twenty years.

**Instruction 10**

Read Box 12.

---

**Box 12**

A transition from an economy protected from competition to an economy that accepts and promotes competition has significant implications. First, firms are obliged to allocate resources more efficiently to increase productivity. Second, domestic firms, when forced to compete internationally, have to develop and mature technologically and managerial. Third, a more competitive economic environment is more sensitive and vulnerable to changes in demand for types and quality of products. As a consequence, it will be more difficult to predict which skills will be needed in the future and for how long. These factors necessitate a more mobile work-force that is flexible in adopting new skills.

Wad D Haddad, 'Globalisation of the economy: the implications for education and skill formation' *Prospects*, Vol. XXVII, No.1, March 1997, p.36

---

It is clear today that the human resource is of paramount importance and knowledge is the critical skill. This heightens the role of education.

*Instruction 11*

Read Boxes 13 and 14.

**Box 13**

In the past comparative advantage was a function of natural-resources endowments and factor proportions (capital-labour ratios). Cotton was grown in the American South because the climate and soil were right. Slavery provided abundant labour. Cotton was spun in New England because it had the capital to harness available waterpower. Each industry had its natural location.

*Consider what are commonly believed to be the seven key industries of the next few decades – microelectronics, biotechnology, the new materials industries, civilian aviation, telecommunications, robots plus machine tools, and computers plus software.* All are brainpower industries. Each could be located anywhere on the face of the globe. Where they will be located depends upon who can organise the brainpower to capture them. *In the century ahead comparative advantage will be man-made.*

Since technology lies behind man-made comparative advantage, research and development becomes critical. In the past the economic winners were those who invented new products. The British in the nineteenth century and the Americans in the twentieth century got rich doing so. But in the twenty-first century sustainable competitive advantage will come much more out of new process technologies and much less out of new product technologies. Reverse engineering has become an art form. New products can easily be reproduced. What used to be primary (inventing new products) becomes secondary, and what used to be secondary (inventing and perfecting new processes) becomes primary.

Lester Thurrow, *Head to Head*. William Morrow & Co. Inc., NY, p. 45

## Box 14

Firms have to be able to use new computer-based CAD-CAM *technologies, employ statistical quality control, manage just-in-time inventories, and operate flexible manufacturing systems. Information technologies have to be integrated into the entire production process,* from initial designs through marketing to final sales and supporting services such as maintenance. *To do this requires the office, the factory, the retail store, and the repair service to have average workers with levels of education and skill that they have never had to have in the past. To employ statistical quality control, every production worker must be taught some simple operations research.* To learn what must be learnt, every worker must have a level of basic mathematics that is far beyond what is achieved by most American high school graduates. Without statistical quality control, today's high-density semiconductor chips cannot be built. They can be invented, but they cannot be built.

Lester Thurrow, *op. cit.*

## Activity 12

1. *Which are the key industries of the future?*

2. *Why are they called brain-based industries?*

3. *How is information technology being integrated into production?*

4. *How can information technology affect management and organisation?*

## Instruction 12

Read Box 15.

---

**Box 15**

First are the modern problem-solving skills required to put things together in unique ways (be they alloys, molecules, semi-conductor chips, software codes, movie scripts, pension portfolios or information) . . .

Next are the skills required to help customers understand their needs and how those needs can best be met by customised products . . . selling and marketing customised products requires having intimate knowledge of a customer's business, where competitive advantage may lie, and how it can be achieved. The key is to identify new problems and possibilities to which the customised product might be applicable. The art of persuasion is replaced by the identification of opportunity. Third are the skills needed to link problem-solvers and problem-identifiers. People in such roles must understand enough about specific technologies and markets to see the potential for new products, raise whatever money is necessary to launch the project, and assemble the right problem-solvers and identifiers to carry it out.

Robert Reich, *The Work of Nations*

---

**Activity 13**

1. *Discuss the range of skills required by the work-force.*

2. *What does this suggest for the provision of education both in quality and quantity?*

---

## Summary

The rise of the new informational economy once more makes education a primary concern for economic growth and development. In fact the connection between education and development which prevailed in the 1960s is now stronger than ever. It is now asserted by writers like Robert Reich and Michael Porter that education determines the possibilities for development in the modern era.

## Suggested reading

### Section 1

Best, Lloyd and Levitt, Kari (1967). *Externally propelled growth in the Caribbean, Selected Essays.* Centre for Developing Area Studies, McGill University.

Cardoso and Faletto (1979). *Dependency and Development in Latin America.* University of California Press.

Inkeles, Alex and Smith, O (1974). *Becoming modern: individual change in six developing countries.* Cambridge, Mass: Harvard University Press.

### Section 2

La Guerre, John (ed.) (1994). *Structural Adjustment Education. Public Policy and Administration in the Caribbean.* School of Continuing Studies, UWI., St. Augustine.

Levitt, Kari (1991). *The Origins and Consequences of Jamaica's Debt Crisis.* Consortium Graduate School of Social Sciences.

Manley, Michael (1987). *Up the Down Escalator.* London: Andre Deutsch.

Samoff, Joel, (ed.). *Coping with Crisis.* Cassell. UNESCO.

Tilak, J B G (1997). 'The effects of adjustment on education: a review of the Asian experience', *Prospects,* Vol. XXXVII No.1, March, pp. 85–107.

Tilak, J B G (1992). 'Education and structural adjustment', *Prospects* 22 (4), No. 8, pp. 407–22.

Tilak, J B G (1989). 'The recession and public investment in education in Latin America', *Journal of Inter-American Studies and World Affairs,* 31 (1–2) (Spring–Summer), pp. 125–46.

### Section 3

Haq, Mabbab-Ul (1995). *Reflection on Human Development.* Oxford: Oxford University Press.

Miller, Errol (1992). *Education for all: Caribbean Perspectives and Imperatives.* IADB Washington, DC.

Tilak, J B G (1992). 'From economic growth to human development: a commentary on recent Indexes of Development', *International Journal of Social Economics,* 19 (2), pp. 31–42.

UNDP: Human Development Reports, 1990–1998.

UNESCO (1995). *Our Creative Diversity.* Report of the World Commission on Culture and Development.

## Section 4

Carvog, Castello *et al.* (1993). *The New Global Economy in the Information Age.* University Park: Pennsylvania State University Press.

Reich, Robert (1991). *The Work of Nations.* New York: Basic Books.

Thurrow, Lester (1992). *Head to Head.* New York: William Morrow & Co. Inc.

Some articles in *Prospects* Vol. XXXVII No.1. March 1997 are also relevant to this section.

# MODULE 2
## Assessing the local educational environment

This module consists of seven sections. Each section gives some stimulus materials to be read, some questions for discussion, and some background and summary points to facilitate understanding. At the end of the sections there is suggested further reading for the module.

Having looked at the international environment and the implications for educational financing in Module 1, it is now necessary to survey the local educational environment to be able to determine the needs of the system and the kinds of interventions necessary in the local educational environment. Scanning the local environment will help to determine, in the light of international trends and national development goals, at which level intervention is required, i.e. preschool, primary, secondary, tertiary, and what kind of intervention is required – teacher training, curriculum development, resources and administrative training or capital expansion.

## SECTION 1

At the end of Section 1 the participant should be able to identify the key policy issues affecting educational planning.

In this and following sections we will clarify the four main issues for policy analysis in setting priorities and programmes for educational development and financing. Policy analysis is the process by which relevant information is provided in order to guide the determination of policy options.

*Instruction 1*

Read Box 1.

---

**Box 1**

**Four main policy issues**

1. The efficiency of the education system must be maximised.

2. The education system must meet the manpower needs of the economy.

3. The education system must respond to individual demand for education.

4. The education system must respond to the needs for social equity in terms of its provisions.

---

**Activity 1**

*Study the four policy issues in Box 1 and reflect on your own country. In setting up an overall policy framework to guide educational expansion, are these the four most critical issues?*

---

We will proceed now to examine each of these four issues and the key measures, indicators and concerns of each in the following four sections.

# SECTION 2

At the end of Section 2 the participant should be able to:

1. Explain internal and external efficiency;

2. Use relevant measures of internal and external efficiency.

Here we take a look at the concepts of efficiency in education.

### Instruction 2

Study Box 2.

---

**Box 2**

**CONCEPTS OF EFFICIENCY IN EDUCATION**

Efficiency is a term used to describe the relationship between inputs and outputs, but because this relationship can be analysed from several perspectives, judgments about efficiency may have to take into account more than one aspect of the relationship. Investment decisions, for example, need to consider both external and internal efficiency. The problem is that educational output is too complex to allow us to adopt a single index of either external or internal efficiency.

As we have already seen, the objectives of society are used to measure external efficiency, which can be judged by the balance between social costs and social benefits, or the extent to which education satisfies manpower and employment needs. More specifically, the external efficiency of schools may be judged by how well schools prepare pupils and students for their roles in society, as indicated by the employment prospects and earnings of students. Such measures depend on external criteria rather than on results entirely within the school.

In contrast, internal efficiency is concerned with the relationship between inputs and outputs within the education system or within individual institutions. Output in this case is measured in relation to internal institutional goals rather than the wider objectives of society. Clearly, the two concepts are closely linked, but it would be possible to envisage a school that was extremely efficient in developing skills and attitudes that were not highly valued in society as a whole. In such circumstances, the criteria of internal and external efficiency would conflict, and the school would be judged to be internally efficient but externally inefficient.

---

In some countries it is possible that schools can claim to be internally efficient, i.e. a large percentage of their students are successful at exams. However, these students may be unprepared for the world of work. There exists, then, conflict between criteria for internal and external efficiency.

## Indicators of Efficiency

Indicators of efficiency are very useful at this point in time where most countries face adverse financial circumstances and the central challenge to educational managers is to find ways to use limited resources more efficiently and effectively. Cost analysis can help educational managers to see the various options and tradeoffs available to them and assess their relative merits and demerits. Cost analysis can reveal waste and inefficiency and alternative ways of deploying resources between levels and types of education.

### Instruction 3

Read Box 3. These are just some of the efficiency or cost indicators that can be used to assess the educational arrangements on the ground.

1. Can you think of other indicators?

**Box 3**
**Efficiency Indicators**

1. Unit costs
   (a) cost per graduate
   (b) cost per classroom
   (c) cost per school
2. Enrolment ratios
3. Attendance rate
4. Dropout rate
5. Repetition rate
6. Teachers' salaries
7. Recurrent costs
8. Capital costs
9. Education costs as percentage of GDP
10. Cost by levels, i.e. preschool, primary, secondary, tertiary.

## Instruction 4

Read Box 4. This is taken from a 1993 World Bank study of the Caribbean.

---

### Box 4

#### Repetition/Attendance/Dropouts

The situation in Haiti and the Dominican Republic appears to be much worse than in English-speaking countries, as Table 2.1 demonstrates. The data shows even distributions of enrolments across primary school classes and relatively low repeaters in both Jamaica and Trinidad. In Haiti and the Dominican Republic, however, enrolments fall substantially and repeater levels are two to three times as high. Apparently only one-third of primary school entrants in Haiti complete the cycle.

**Table 2.1. Haiti, Dominican Republic, Jamaica and Trinidad: Indicators of Primary School Efficiency**

|  | Haiti | Dominican Rep. | Jamaica | Trinidad |
|---|---|---|---|---|
| Percent distribution of primary enrolment |  |  |  |  |
| Grade 1 | 41 | 35 | 21 | 21 |
| Grade 2 | 20 | 19 | 20 | 21 |
| Grade 3 | 16 | 17 | 20 | 20 |
| Grade 4 | 13 | 15 | 20 | 19 |
| Grade 5 | 10 | 14 | 19 | 19 |
| Repeaters as a percentage of total enrolments |  |  |  |  |
| 1980 | 21 | 18 | 4 | 4 |
| 1985 | 10 | 13 | 4 | 5 |
| Percentage of primary intake reaching terminal grade |  |  |  |  |
| 1975 | — | — | 75 | — |
| 1985 | 32 | — | — | — |

*Source:* Lockheed and Verspoor, 1990

In summary, as the above data highlight, many countries in the Caribbean region experience high rates of grade repetition. While the dropout rates in English-speaking countries appear to be low, in some countries, particularly the Dominican Republic and Haiti, school desertion also is high. The usual argument in favour of repetition is that it is preferable to make a low-achieving child repeat a class to ensure that all material in that grade is mastered, rather than allowing the child to proceed to the next grade. However, repetition has many disadvantages. It encourages dropout, as the repeating child may become demoralised, particularly as he/she inevitably must repeat some material already mastered. Further, his parents may decide that the opportunity costs of schooling are too great.

*Caribbean Region – Access, Quality and Efficiency in Education.* Washington DC: World Bank, 1993, p. 67

### Activity 3

1. *Discuss the possible implications for educational policy.*

2. *How does it compare with your country?*

## Instruction 5

Read Box 5.

---

### Box 5
### Recurrent Unit Costs by Education Level

Interpreting comparative data on expenditures by distinct education levels across countries requires some yardstick. One useful measure is the difference in unit costs of providing primary, secondary and tertiary education in the Caribbean, the most recent estimates of which are presented in Table 2.2.

**Table 2.2. Caribbean – Recurrent Government Education Expenditures: Unit Cost per Level (in US$ Equivalent)**

| Country/Level | Primary | Secondary | Tertiary | University |
|---|---|---|---|---|
| Antigua | 251 | 423 | 1287 | — |
| Dominica | 250 | 449 | 1201 | — |
| Grenada | 160 | 256 | 807 | — |
| St. Kitts | 221 | 313 | 1604 | — |
| St. Vincent | 213 | 1783 | — | |
| St. Lucia | 209 | 579 | 1873 | — |
| OECS Countries Average | 217 | 382 | 1426 | — |
| Bahamas | 640 | 1010 | 1200 | — |
| Belize | 157 | 362 | 699 | — |
| Barbados | 672 | 913 | 1200 | — |
| Guyana | 26 | 54 | 146 | 858 |
| Jamaica | 101 | 257 | 639 | 5138 |
| Trinidad | 596 | 811 | — | 10510 |
| Haiti | 44 | 101 | — | — |
| Suriname | 445 | 911 | 3156 | 5538 |

Other than Grenada, with a relatively low cost structure, close similarities appear to exist across the OECS countries in the unit costs of education. On average, primary schooling costs US$217 per student, secondary US$382 and tertiary (non-university) US$1,426. Substantial variation exists between costs, by level, among the other English-speaking countries, however. Although unit costs at the primary level average US$366 within this group of countries, the range is vast, from US$26 in Guyana to US$672 in Barbados. At the secondary level, costs within this country grouping tend to be two to three times higher than those in the OECS countries. The notable exceptions are Belize, with costs similar to the OECS countries, and Jamaica and Guyana in which average costs are lower. At the tertiary non-university level, also, only Jamaica, Belize and Guyana are exceptions, with other English-speaking countries having unit costs similar to the OECS group. Estimated expenditures per student in higher education (including overseas scholarships) also point to differences between Jamaica and Guyana and the other campus countries.

*Source:* See Statistical Appendix (I) of The World Bank Report

---

## Activity 4

1. *What might contribute to the disparity in unit costs between territories?*
2. *What contributes to the disparity between levels?*
3. *What policy implications does this structure of cost imply for expansion of the system?*

---

### Instruction 6

Read Boxes 6 and 7.

---

## Box 6

### Table 2.3. Caribbean – Recurrent Government Education Expenditure as a Share of GNP, 1984–88 (per cent)

|                      | 1984 | 1985 | 1986 | 1987 | 1988 |
|----------------------|------|------|------|------|------|
| **Country Expenditure** |      |      |      |      |      |
| Antigua              | 2.5  | 2.2  | 2.8  | 2.4  | —    |
| Dominica             | 5.7  | 5.2  | 5.3  | 5.1  | 4.9  |
| Grenada              | 6.4  | 6.1  | 5.5  | 4.6  | 4.6  |
| St. Kitts            | 4.1  | 4.0  | 4.0  | 3.8  | 3.5  |
| St. Lucia            | 7.2  | 7.5  | 7.2  | 7.8  | 8.6  |
| St. Vincent          | 5.9  | 5.7  | 5.8  | 6.0  | 6.1  |
| Belize               | 4.3  | 4.4  | 5.3  | 4.4  | 3.9  |
| Bahamas              | —    | 4.6  | —    | 4.3  | —    |
| Barbados             | 5.5  | 6.0  | 5.3  | 5.9  | 5.4  |
| Guyana               | —    | —    | —    | —    | 2.9  |
| Jamaica              | 5.2  | 5.4  | 4.7  | 4.1  | 4.8  |
| Trinidad             | 5.1  | 5.0  | 5.0  | 5.6  | —    |
| Haiti                | 1.0  | 1.0  | 0.9  | 1.4  | —    |
| Dominican Rep.       | 1.7  | 1.5  | 1.4  | 1.3  | 1.3  |
| Suriname             | 11.0 | 11.1 | 9.9  | 9.6  | 9.0  |

Note: Expenditures for the Dominican Republic are current and capital

*Source:* See Statistical Appendix (I)(Caribbean Region, *op. cit.*)

## Box 7

**Table 2.4 Caribbean – Fiscal Education Spending as a Share of Total Government Recurrent Expenditure, 1984–88 (percent)**

|                 | 1984 | 1985 | 1986 | 1987 | 1988 |
|-----------------|------|------|------|------|------|
| Antigua         | 12.6 | 11.5 | 12.5 | 11.5 | —    |
| Dominica        | 18.9 | 17.7 | 19.0 | 19.4 | 19.1 |
| Grenada         | 19.8 | 19.1 | 18.6 | 15.7 | 17.5 |
| St. Kitts       | 19.3 | 19.2 | 20.0 | 17.7 | 17.0 |
| St. Lucia       | 25.1 | 24.3 | 23.7 | 24.1 | 24.1 |
| St. Vincent     | 21.3 | 20.7 | 22.4 | 25.2 | 20.6 |
| Belize          | 20.2 | 19.8 | 22.3 | 20.7 | 19.6 |
| Bahamas         | —    | 24.5 | —    | 24.1 | —    |
| Barbados        | 21.1 | 21.7 | 20.4 | 20.5 | 19.3 |
| Guyana          | —    | 11.3 | 10.3 | 7.0  | 9.0  |
| Jamaica         | 16.6 | 14.5 | 16.2 | 18.1 | 16.7 |
| Trinidad        | 17.1 | —    | 17.4 | 18.3 | —    |
| Haiti           | 10.3 | 10.0 | 10.0 | 15.4 | —    |
| Dominican Rep.* | 3.6  | 11.3 | 9.9  | 8.0  | 9.1  |
| Suriname        | 25.6 | 24.9 | 22.8 | 26.0 | 25.7 |

*Expenditures for the Dominican Republic are both current and capital.
*Source:* See Statistical Appendix (I)

## Activity 5

1. How do the countries of the Caribbean compare in the percentage of the budget dedicated to education?
   How do they compare in the percentage of GDP dedicated to education?

2. What do these trends reveal when one considers the need to improve education in these territories?

## External efficiency

In considering the external efficiency of the education system the policy maker has to consider the outcomes of education. Do the school leavers get jobs? Do they have the right types and combination of skills? Are they able to perform in the workplace?

## Instruction 7

Study Box 8.

# Box 8

## Table 2.5. Caribbean – Probabilities of Different Levels of Educational Achievement across the English-speaking Countries

| | Antigua | Barbados | Belize | Dominica | Grenada | Guyana | Jamaica | St. Kitts | St. Lucia | St. Vincent | Trinidad |
|---|---|---|---|---|---|---|---|---|---|---|---|
| Enter Primary 1 | 100 | 100 | 100 | 100 | 100 | 100 | 100 | 100 | 100 | 100 | 100 |
| Complete Primary | 98 | 100 | 59 | 93 | 95 | 80 | 85 | 97 | 93 | 98 | 100 |
| Enter Post Primary | 43 | 4 | ** | ** | 48 | 54 | 32 | 4 | 50 | 39 | 23 |
| Enter Secondary | 55 | 96 | 35 | 25 | 45 | 26 | 53 | 93 | 23 | 39 | 70 |
| Complete Secondary | ** | ** | 21 | ** | 38 | 26 | 53 | ** | 21 | ** | 65 |
| CXC Stream | 55 | ** | 21 | 25 | *** | 26 | 32 | 43 | 21 | 35 | 65 |
| CXC English | 28 | ** | 8 | 7 | 12 | 3 | 8 | 18 | 9 | 13 | (24) |
| CXC Math | 18 | ** | 6 | 7 | 8 | 3 | 7 | 15 | 7 | 11 | (19) |
| 4 + CXC | 4 | 8 | 2 | 2 | 3 | 2 | 3 | 4 | 2 | 4 | 5 |
| Take 'A' Levels | ** | 5 | 2 | 3 | 5 | *** | 3 | 5 | 2 | 6 | 7 |
| Pass 2+ 'A' Levels | ** | ** | 1 | 1 | 1 | *** | ** | 2 | 1 | 1 | 2 |
| Enter other Tertiary Institution | ** | 42 | 5 | 3 | 3 | 6 | 7 | 9 | 4 | 4 | 10 |
| Enter Caribbean University | 1.5 | 3 | 0.25 | 0.25 | 1 | 2 | 2 | 2 | 1 | 0.5 | 3 |

Notes   1. The probabilities are based on each 100 primary entrants.
   2. ** indicates a data gap
   3. *** indicates not applicable
   4. CXC is the Caribbean Examinations Council.
   5. 'A' Level is the General Certificate of Education Advanced Level which is required for entry to U.W.I.

*Source:* Caribbean Region., *op. cit.*

33

## Activity 6

1. What does it suggest about the achievements in the Caribbean at the primary level?

2. Is our output at the secondary level adequate?

3. What does this table say about the tertiary level?

4. What implications are there for policy?

We must keep in mind that at the turn of the century we need to produce a larger cohort of university graduates. In addition, the level of skills required for certain jobs will not be forthcoming and this will worsen the situation of structural unemployment.

Another set of outcomes required in the Caribbean focuses on the need to prepare children so that the problems of drug addiction, teenage pregnancy, youth delinquency and crime would be reduced.

At this stage we have considered the indicators required to determine the internal and external efficiency of an educational system. We have done so by examining the indicators for the Caribbean.

## SECTION 3

At the end of Section 3 the participant should be able to:

1. Explain the concept of manpower planning;

2. Identify some problems with this approach.

### Does the educational system satisfy the manpower needs of the country?

The question of satisfying manpower needs is the second key question the policy maker must deal with.

## Instruction 8

Read Box 9.

---

### Box 9

Although fraught with dangers and besieged by criticism, the idea that a country's future manpower structure can be predicted and the forecasts used as a basis for planning the scale and type of education investment has remained popular. The most popular method sets out to use projected output targets for each sector in the economy in order to derive manpower and education targets for each industry or sector.

---

### Activity 7

1. Can you see dangers in this process?

2. What assumptions have to be made about the future for each sector as far as technology and prices of inputs and outputs?

---

'Despite the weaknesses however, the overall conclusion to date is that manpower projections are not bad in themselves if they are carried out realistically – that is, if it is recognised that they are subject to wide margins of error and do not reflect hard and fast requirements of economic growth' (Psacharopoulos and Woodhall, 1986). When complemented by other studies of the labour market, manpower projections can give policy makers a sense of the needs education must satisfy. While the practical application of the manpower approach has revealed a number of flaws, the broad logic of the manpower approach is extremely sound. The development of human resources through the educational system is an important prerequisite for economic growth and a good investment of scarce resources, provided the pattern and quality of educational output is geared to the economy's manpower needs.

Such studies, along with the manpower forecasts, will determine where there is excess demand and where scarcities exist. Where does unemployment exist? How long have graduates taken to get jobs on the labour market? All of this will help to determine whether the forces of demand and supply on the labour market can deal with possible excesses and shortages.

# SECTION 4

At the end of Section 4 the participant should be able to explain the use of private demand in educational planning.

**Instruction 9**

Read Box 10.

---

### Box 10

**Responding to private demand**
Because the terms social demand and private demand are often used interchangeably, confusion sometimes arises in discussion of demand. The total number of pupils or students enrolled in an education system is the result of a series of private investment decisions. Together, however, these private decisions constitute social demand. It has been suggested in some developed countries that social demand should be the criterion for educational investment decisions.

Psacharopoulos and Woodhall, 1986, p.108

---

### Activity 8

*What do you understand by the social demand approach to educational planning?*

---

In addition to demographic trends, promotion, repetition and dropout rates, a knowledge of private demand is essential to be able to forecast enrolments accurately. The aggregation of the sum of individual demands constitutes what is called the social demand for education under the prevailing cultural, economic and political circumstances. If there are fewer classrooms and places than there are serious candidates to occupy them, one can say that social demand exceeds supply.

Coombs (1970) identifies three criticisms of the social demand approach. Firstly, 'it ignores the larger national problem of resource allocation and implicitly assumes that no matter how many resources go to education this is their best use for national development'. Secondly, 'it ignores the character and pattern of manpower needed by the economy'. Thirdly, 'it tends to over-stimulate popular demand, to underestimate costs, and to lead to a thin spreading of resources over too many students.'

Read Box 11.

---

**Box 11**

Economic analysis of the private demand for education must take into account a number of factors that help to determine demand such as:

– private costs of education including both earnings foregone and fees

– other direct costs such as expenditure on books or materials

– gender and region

– expected increase in lifetime earnings

– level of personal disposable income

– unemployment rates

---

**Activity 9**

1. *Could you show how each of the factors listed above affects the private demand for education?*

2. *Are there cultural reasons why girls may sometimes not be sent to school as readily as boys? At low income levels some families may not be able to afford the incidental costs of schooling. In some cultures children may be kept at home to work the fields.*

---

## Private rate of return

If we can estimate how individuals value an investment in education, then we can project what type of demand for education would exist. Reducing this estimate to a rate allows us to discern the strength of that demand.

## Instruction 11

Study Box 12.

---

**Box 12**

**Rate of Return for a 3-Year Degree Programme**

| Direct Costs | Yr 1 | Yr 2 | Yr 3 |
|---|---|---|---|
| (a) University fees | — | — | — |
| (b) Accommodation | — | — | — |
| (c) Books | — | — | — |
| **Indirect Costs** | | | |
| (a) Transport | — | — | — |
| (b) Daily living expenses | — | — | — |
| (c) Photocopying | — | — | — |
| **Income Foregone** | — | — | — |
| Total | xxx | xxx | xxx |
| Benefit | Yr 1 | Yr 2 | Yr 3 |
| Expected Earnings | — | — | — |

---

This is a very simplified approach to estimating a rate of return. From the example it is clear that we need to cost the degree programme over the three years. If we can then establish the stream of earnings the student is likely to earn after qualifying, we can infer that the bigger the expected earnings are compared to projected costs, the higher is the private rate of return. The rate of return for different occupations or fields will convey to the educational planner the strength of demand in that field, as well as the possibility of making students in those areas where private rates of return are high bear some of the costs of education.

# SECTION 5

At the end of Section 5 the participant should be able to:

1. Determine the state of inequity in his or her own country;
2. Advance indicators of inequality;
3. Suggest educational interventions.

## The question of equity

The fourth question which policy makers must address in an assessment of the local educational environment is the question of equity. Equity is a crucial consideration for continued stability. Equity does not mean equality. It may be more practically defined as 'unequal treatment for unequal partners'.

### Instruction 12

Read Box 13.

---

**Box 13**

Four questions in particular need to be examined if we are to determine the effects of educational investment on equity.

1. How are educational resources and facilities distributed among different areas or groups?
2. What are the effects of government subsidies for education on the distribution of total income or welfare?
3. Can educational investment be used to redistribute wealth, income, and opportunities between rich and poor?
4. How effective is education as a redistribute tool?

Psacharopoulos and Woodhall, 1986, p. 244

---

**Activity 10**

1. *What indicators of equity is it necessary to focus on?*
2. *How does your country fare by these indicators?*
3. *Compare access to education in your country by gender, ethnicity, location, income level.*
4. *How have redistributive policies worked in your country?*

---

## Instruction 13

Read Box 14. These findings certainly provide evidence that educational provision can affect income distribution.

---

**Box 14**

The general conclusion of various studies appear to show that:

(a) Education may raise the overall level of income and thus reduce the absolute level of poverty.

(b) It may change the dispersion of income.

(c) It may open up new opportunities for the children of the poor and thus act as a vehicle for social mobility.

(d) Alternatively, if participation is confined to the children of the rich, education may simply transmit intergenerational inequality.

(e) The pattern of financing, in particular the extent of subsidies or fees may redistribute income.

(f) If certain groups obtain higher rewards from their education than others then inequality is perpetuated.

(g) Education may interact with fertility, morality, health, nutrition and other aspects of development that affect income distribution.

Psacharopoulos and Woodhall, op. cit., p. 267

---

**Activity 11**

1. What is the state of income distribution in your country?

2. How can a change in access affect the state of inequality?

3. How can a change in subsidies work to remove inequality?

4. How can the implementation of user fees affect distribution?

---

It is important to note that overall social policy is necessary to tackle the problem of income inequality. Educational financing and provision is one tool which can also contribute to this purpose. The impact of educational interventions can be limited by certain barriers. For example, when there is race or gender discrimination practised in the labour market, more educational provision does not resolve the problem.

# SECTION 6

At the end of Section 6 the participant should be able to use all the concerns of the previous sections to assess the local educational environment.

## Assessing the context and setting priorities

Having addressed the previous policy questions we can now assess the local educational context. Where does inefficiency exist? Where does inequality exist? What is the projected demand for various skills and occupations? What is the private demand in different areas? At what level is intervention necessary – pre-primary, primary, secondary, tertiary? Do we need to expand enrolment or concentrate on effective delivery? Do we need to emphasise teacher training, administrative development, school feeding, transport or other support services. What is the appropriate mix of options required to suit our needs at this point in time?

*Instruction 14*

Read Box 15.

---

**Box 15**

**Framework for policy analysis**

1. After analysing the context and identifying weaknesses and needs, keeping in mind the constraints of resources and outlook of the government of the day, the policy makers must set priorities and options. The full range of possibilities must be represented.

2. Policy makers must be mindful of the differences between policy analysis and decision making. Policy analysis is broad. Policy will set up a framework for decision making, but decision making will be affected and conditioned by other unquantifiable factors.

3. Policy analysis must always warn of the cost of inaction.

4. Policy analysis must at times engage the political environment. This may broaden the range of options.

---

## Activity 12

1. Examine any education plan for your country. Is the policy framework set out at the beginning?

2. In this plan what is the relationship between the policy framework and the action plan?

3. What mix of intervention strategies does your plan recommend?

4. How does the plan justify the mix of options recommended?

5. Do you agree with the assessment of the local educational environment?

# SECTION 7

At the end of Section 7 the participant should be able to articulate a theory of school improvement which would inform the educational response.

### Instruction 15

Read Box 16.

## Box 16

Having analysed the local educational environment and having determined its weaknesses and strengths, the policy makers must come up with a mix of options for the system as a whole. The mix of options would be strongly influenced by the theory of school improvement possessed by the policy makers. What do people mean by a good school or a bad school? Are schools seen as important vehicles for social change? What benefits are there in a decentralised school environment? What concept of education do the policy makers wish to institute?

## Activity 13

1. How would options for change be affected at the level of ministry, school, teacher if there is a fundamental thrust to decentralisation?

2. How would options for change be affected if education emphasised process rather than achievement by exams?

3. How would options for change be affected if there is a renewed emphasis on the power of schools as social agents of change?

## Suggested reading

*Caribbean Region – Access, Quality and Efficiency in Education* (1992). World Bank.

*Country Study.* Washington DC.

Coombs, Phillip H. *What is Educational Planning?* International Institute for Educational Planning. UNESCO.

Davies, B and Ellison, L (1977). *School Leadership for the 21st Century.* London: Routledge & Kegan Paul.

Psacharopoulos, George and Woodhall, Maureen (1986). *Education for Development.* World Bank Publisher. Oxford: Oxford University Press.

Ruscoe, G C (1980). *The Conditions for Success in Educational Planning.* International Institute for Educational Planning. UNESCO.

# MODULE 3
# Planning the financing of education

## Overview

Modules 1 and 2 helped you to develop a comprehensive idea of how both the global environment and the local context conspire to constrain and influence the financing of education. It is now time to focus on the system itself to get a general idea of its operations, and its financial demands. In Section 1 of this module we are going to take a closer look at indicators or descriptors in use that can throw light on how the system may be operating. The question we are trying to answer is this: *How do planners know that they are financing their education system adequately?* The descriptors or indicators become useful tools in determining how the system is functioning at present levels of financing.

Having explored the indices that help us to determine if we are financing education adequately, we then go on to Section 2, which considers whether we have been raising the money in the most efficient and equitable ways. Various alternatives are examined which help to widen the frameworks governing how educational financing has been conceptualised and sourced in the past.

## SECTION 1

### Objectives

At the end of Section 1, the participants should be able to:

1. Analyse the reasons why governments take an interest in education.

2. Identify important indicators of flows, distributions and stocks in an education system.

3. Infer from these indicators information about the various levels of the education system.

4. Evaluate the strengths and weaknesses of such indicators.

5. Justify recommendations for adequate levels of financing to maintain and improve the education system.

A pertinent question at the start of this module, on which participants can reflect, is *why should governments take an interest in education at all?* In much of the Third World we have inherited colonial educational structures and, since independence, nationalist governments have continued to build upon this system and expand it. We have gone through a period in the 1960s and 1970s when human capital and modernisation theories sought to convince governments that education was the key to economic development. Today, that has been exposed as a myth. However, education continues to be a priority with governments. This module will provide some answers to the question posed above. You will also be interested in the sorts of answers given by personnel, especially from the Ministry of Education and that of Finance. Exploring this question can be worthwhile.

---

**Activity 1**

*Why should governments take an interest in education? Research this issue in the following ways:*

1. *Write down your answers to the above question.*

2. *Pose the question to personnel of the Ministries of Education and Finance.*

3. *Peruse national policy papers such as plans of education or budget speeches.*

*Organise the responses into categories. What are the implications inherent in your findings? Discuss your findings with those of other participants.*

---

The actual reasons explaining government involvement in education may differ substantially in different parts of the world. However, once that interest is there, and that means money is invested in the system, governments need to know through various mechanisms how well they are doing. This is usually done through indicators of various sorts and it is to the utility of these indicators that much of this module is devoted.

The appropriations bill of national governments allocates funds to education using criteria which are based on an understanding of the international and local contexts of financing. Budgetary allocation within education itself is often organised in ways that take cognisance of policies to which governments have already given their approval, for example expansion of basic education, apparently without a holistic view of how the entire system is performing. It is mandatory, especially in times of financial stringency, that planners in education and finance have detailed knowledge of the operations of the entire system to provide a basis for determining whether it is being optimally financed. Doing it solely the other way, i.e. allocating funds based on projects and reforms previously agreed upon, relies on a kind of blind faith that everything outside those sectors is functioning well. Indicators provide evidence and clues that tell what the situation is and how it is changing.

This activity is designed to allow participants to identify and infer educational and financing information from a wide array of indicators.

---

### Activity 2

*Below is a general list of the most common indicators that are presumed to throw light on the relationships, stocks, flows and distributions within the education system. Attempt to reorganise the list under five categories that you believe may be important in assessing the financing of education.*

- *Students' examination performance*
- *Student-teacher ratios*
- *Repetition rates*
- *Rates of population growth*
- *Numbers of teachers leaving*
- *Migration trends*
- *Teacher stocks*
- *Enrolment ratios*
- *Teacher wage bill*
- *Illiteracy rates*
- *Enrolment in, and costs of, different curriculum areas*
- *Enrolment in different types of schools*
- *Numbers of dropouts at each level of schooling and type of school*
- *Structure of the national population by age and sex*
- *Student enrolment and performance by gender, ethnicity, religion, and geographic area*

---

One way of approaching this exercise is to reflect on what categories of information you would consider important to have in hand in making judgements about the adequacy of how the system is being financed. Immediately, you realise that one must have a fairly precise idea of:

1. Numbers of students;

2. Numbers of teachers within the system;

3. How those numbers will change in the next few years;

4. Whether all groups are accessing education equally;

5. Whether invested resources are being utilised efficiently.

The reorganised list should look something like this (some indicators may overlap categories):

1. **Student Enrolment** – enrolment ratios, enrolment in different types of schools

2. **Teacher Supply** – teacher stocks, teacher wage bill, numbers of teachers leaving, student-teacher ratios

3. **Demographic factors** – structure of the national population by age and sex, rates of population growth, migration trends, student enrolment and performance by geographic area

4. **Equity** – student enrolment and performance by gender, ethnicity, religion, and geographic area; enrolment in different types of schools; illiteracy rates

5. **Efficiency considerations** – students' examination performance, repetition rates, numbers of dropouts at each level of schooling and type of school, enrolment in and costs of different curriculum areas, numbers of teachers leaving, enrolment in different types of schools, illiteracy rates.

**Gross Enrolment Ratios** are obtained by dividing the total number of students enrolled in a level or stage of education by the wider population of that age group corresponding to that level or stage. For example:

$$\frac{\textit{Number enrolled in primary schools}}{\textit{Number of children of primary school age}}$$

This indicates information on the numbers in each stage or level (for example, primary, secondary and tertiary) who are in school, as well as the non-schooling gap for those stages or levels. The spread of children in each level, graduates from each level and the approximate attrition taking place as students progress throughout the system also becomes known. This indicator, because it assumes that persons enrolled in schools must be of primary school age (in many countries 5–11 years), may approach totals that exceed the number of children in the country of that age group. A refinement of this is the net enrolment rate calculated by dividing:

$$\frac{\textit{Number of pupils enrolled only of primary school age}}{\textit{Number of children of primary school age}}$$

In assessing the financing of the system, questions tend to centre around whether the enrolment ratios at primary, secondary and tertiary levels are acceptable given the resources of the country and its development plans and prospects. For example, Universal Primary Education (UPE) is a widespread goal for many developing countries and financing decisions may have to prioritise the primary level before considering expanding enrolments ratios on a similar scale in the secondary and tertiary sectors. To gauge whether the financing of the education system is adequate, comparisons are often made to countries of similar income and endowment, as well as to others considered to be more developed.

## Box 1

### Table 3.1. Gross Enrolment Ratios by Level of Education in Selected Countries in 1990

| Country | Gross enrolment ratios % | | |
|---|---|---|---|
| *Developing countries* | Primary | Secondary | Tertiary |
| Sub-Saharan Africa | 66.7 | 17.5 | 1.9 |
| Arab states | 83.4 | 52.7 | 12.6 |
| Latin America/Caribbean | 109.9 | 57.6 | 18.7 |
| Eastern Asia/Oceania | 120.0 | 53.3 | 6.1 |
| Southern Asia | 88.4 | 38.4 | 8.9 |
| *Developed countries* | | | |
| North America | 102.0 | 98.9 | 70.4 |
| Asia/Oceania | 102.0 | 96.8 | 32.8 |
| Europe/former USSR | 102.0 | 93.1 | 27.3 |

NB The intake exceeds 100 per cent where enrolment data include children who are below or above primary school age and are repeating various grades.

*Source:* Reimers and Tiburcio, 1993, p.29

**Enrolment in different types of schools**, especially different types of secondary and tertiary institutions, has been an important indicator in the past, for manpower planning purposes. Manpower planning uses several techniques to match the output of schools over a period, for example the next ten years, with the number and kinds of employment opportunities that would arise in that time on the labour market. Similarly today, assessments of the financing of education focus on whether the heaviest financial outlay is in the kinds of education presently in demand by the labour market.

For example, the traditional concept of education is gradually changing to accommodate an understanding that a general education, that is one having a large component of literacy, numeracy, computer and communication skills, may be more useful in today's world. If it is found that large sums are still supporting a specialised technical-vocational programme in secondary schools, a legacy of the human capital paradigm, then the understanding is that the system is being inappropriately financed.

**Teacher supply:** Any discussion of teacher costs must include recurrent costs. These refer to all expenditure that is disbursed in the short term, i.e. over a budgetary year and include teacher salaries, as well as the maintenance and utility supplies and other services needed by the schools every day. Recurrent costs are often contrasted with capital expenditure which is the heavy financial outlay usually carded for building plant or purchasing expensive equipment and machinery.

**Teacher stocks** provide information on whether there are enough teachers to run the system. The planner must have an overall perspective of what the present teaching stock is like. For example, the proportion of older to younger teachers allows one to be able to forecast how many will leave through retirement and therefore how many, and in what subject areas, recruits will be necessary. This will help to avoid the problem of teacher shortages.

**The teacher wage bill** will also be accurately determined if the teacher stock is known. The financing of the education system must allow for an increase in the bill even though recruits have not entered. Teachers earn increased remuneration through seniority so that salaries and unit costs increase as the teaching population grows older. Keeping costs down may entail encouraging early retirement and maintaining a balanced ratio of older to younger teachers.

**The numbers of teachers leaving the profession** is a difficult indicator to forecast. In response to Structural Adjustment Policies in many developing countries, teachers have had their wages cut and various strategies have been devised to encourage them to retire early. Some may stay on but it is questionable whether in such a climate they, or new recruits, are able to deliver quality instruction.

---

**Box 2**

**The Degradation of the Teaching Environment**

Cuts in the real level of teachers' incomes result in low morale in the profession and reduced motivation and effectiveness, with serious implications for school quality. In addition, teachers may be forced to take on second jobs or activities, often leading to increased absenteeism and to reduced time for preparing classes, correcting papers and being available for students. The erosion of income also leads to trained staff leaving the profession. Scientific, mathematical and technical subjects are particularly affected.

As a result of both lower wages and degradation of working conditions, the attraction of teaching as a career has been considerably reduced. UNESCO's *Statistical Yearbook 1991* indicates a declining proportion of students enrolled in teacher training at the second level of education. Between 1980 and 1989, enrolment in teacher training as a percentage of total enrolment declined from 7.2 to 6.6 per cent in Africa and from 4.1 to 3.2 per cent in Latin America.

An option used to cut back on teacher costs has been to increase the proportion of young, inexperienced and temporary teachers, with the effect of reducing the average salary paid. Using untrained teachers in countries where large numbers are already without qualification is unlikely to contribute to the quality of the system. In Costa Rica, for example, better educated teachers have been gradually replaced by aspirants, high school graduates without adequate training. At the secondary level, these aspirants represented 23.9 per cent of the teaching force in 1990, up from 9.7 per cent three years earlier.

*Source:* Adapted from Reimers and Tiburcio, 1993, pp. 45–46

---

**Student-teacher ratios** are calculated by dividing the total number of students in a school or type of school by the total number of teachers teaching them. Increasing this ratio reduces overall costs. If enrolments increase relative to teacher stock, then more students will be educated at the same cost. A few students can be admitted to a class over the normal maximum, without any rise in costs. Planners bent on maximising costs, though, need to be aware of the threats to quality education in very large classes, such as upwards of 40 students. Financing the system adequately will therefore also involve decision making that seeks to minimise those threats – for example, expansion of enrolments may not necessarily involve increasing the student-teacher ratios in traditional classrooms.

---

### Box 3

**Secondary School Expansion**

A more radical approach to achieving a major expansion in secondary education would be to increase the use of distance-education methods using a combination of written materials, radio broadcasts and correspondence techniques. A combination of self-study and radio broadcasts could be supplemented by supervised study in community centres, secondary schools, tertiary institutions and extramural centres.

In countries with low progression ratios to secondary education, distance education could be used to increase educational opportunities for those who leave school after three years of post-primary education. For the unemployed it could be organised on a full-time basis; for those who work, on a part-time basis. Governments may wish to encourage the establishment of private correspondence schools. Other options are the use of secondary schools (many of which close in the afternoons and evenings) and the strengthening of continuing education departments in tertiary colleges.

*Source:* World Bank, 1993, p. 104

---

## Demographic Factors

**The structure of the national population by age and sex** constitutes basic data that any assessment of the financing of the education system must take into account. These statistics provide information on the size of the school age population in different age ranges. Dynamic factors can alter this structure so that the levels of enrolment in primary schools, for example, from one five-year period to another, may differ considerably. Hence, financing the system adequately in one plan period with 500 primary schools, may not necessarily mean that this remains so if birth rates decline.

**Rates of population growth** can keep planners abreast of how enrolment figures are likely to change. If birth rates decline, then five or six years from that date, primary schools will have a reduced intake; twelve years from that date, junior secondary education will also suffer a similar fate. Building many schools to accommodate the school age population now may pose problems five years later, when expensive capital outlay remains under-utilised A fall in enrolment does not necessarily mean that costs will fall, as the same number of teachers may continue to be employed and recurrent expenses in the form of electricity, water and building maintenance continue as before.

However, the more common problem in developing countries is the continuing high rates of population growth. School building is still far behind what is considered necessary for universal primary education. An assessment of whether the system is being adequately financed must consider not only those enrolled but also the extent of the shortfall in provision.

**Migration trends** call into question the heavy investment by governments in all levels of education. Emigration of highly educated manpower represents significant losses in terms of money invested in people and the potential benefits they could have brought to their country as a result of their advanced training.

---

**Box 4**

**Education and Development – Emigration**

A widespread response to high unemployment and low income levels in the Caribbean has been emigration. In recent decades, the proportion of the Caribbean population voluntarily emigrating each year has been higher than that of any of the regions of the world. While many migrants are very young, much of this emigration has been concentrated among the most highly trained segments of the population. In Jamaica, for example, between 1980 and 1986, the loss of skilled labour through emigration was equal to half the graduates produced by national training institutions over that period in the respective disciplines. A consequence of such high levels of emigration is lower social rates of return to investment in education and training. To a certain extent, local demand for education and training in the Caribbean is linked to anticipated labour market opportunities in North America. Hence, an important issue facing most Caribbean governments amid such high emigration is the appropriate mix of financing for human capital investments, especially at the post-secondary education level, given that individual returns on such investments often significantly exceed those accruing to the state.

*Source:* World Bank, 1993, p. xv

---

**Student enrolment and performance by geographic area** in developing countries show marked differences between urban and rural communities. A certain minimum guaranteed enrolment is necessary to justify the costs of building a secondary school, so urban areas tend to have better provision. The costs are higher than for primary schools because of the specialised curricula needing higher paid subject teachers and a variety of resources. Unit costs are also higher in rural areas where the teacher-pupil ratio may be lower than that in the urban environment.

---

### Activity 3

*Student performance in rural schools tends to be lower than that of students in towns. Consider the following scenarios in relation to what obtains in your own country:*

- *A dearth of highly qualified secondary school teachers;*

- *A high percentage of student unpunctuality and irregularity;*

- *High opportunity costs;*

- *The curriculum in many rural areas offers agricultural courses, but there is low enrolment and a high failure rate.*

*Make a case for adequate financing of rural education in your country and identify relevant organisations that may be of help.*

---

### Equity

Equity considers whether all students are being treated fairly in the system. Financing the education system adequately involves analysing the experiences of different social groups. Just as rural students may suffer inequities, so too might social groups that differ because of gender, religion, ethnicity or some type of handicap. In many developing countries females were admitted late into education and in some countries they are still excluded for various reasons. Yet it has been shown that the benefits that accrue from expanding female enrolments far outweigh the increased expense.

**Box 5**

**Female Literacy and Development**

Increasing national and international concern over the persistence of female illiteracy has been due in part to the steady accumulation of research on its many different implications for the processes of social change and economic development. Besides a focus on the vital role that women play in agriculture and rural development in many countries, attention has also focused on the implications of female illiteracy for population growth and health, and on the relationship between the mother's literacy and education of the child. In the latter connection, the idea of 'family literacy' has been gaining ground in some countries with the realisation that most children spend more time in their years up to adolescence with their family, and especially their mother, than with any other educational 'medium' including school, and that if children have difficulty in reading it is often because their mothers do too. It has been said that the family is 'the world's smallest school'.

*Source:* UNESCO, 1993, p. 28

Many developing countries are ethnically diverse and the planner must be especially vigilant in ensuring that the education system is not inadvertently favouring one social group over another. This is a complex scenario, particularly when international standards and indicators tend to discriminate among the various sectors of a population. One case is the definition of literacy.

**Box 6**

**Equity and Linguistic Diversity**

Since the celebration of International Literacy Year (1990) and the holding of the World Conference on Education for All (Jomtien, 1990) there has been a greater awareness of the whole complex of cultural, social and economic factors associated with the persistence of illiteracy in both developed and developing countries. The question of language is becoming recognised as central. National literacy goals cannot be defined in a meaningful way without explicit reference to the language (or languages) in which the literacy is to be acquired.

International indicators of linguistic diversity have not yet been developed; not all national censuses collect the basic information. The two regions – sub-Saharan Africa and Southern Asia – which have the highest concentrations of illiteracy both have very complex language situations, although in every region there are countries where the population needs to acquire an understanding of more than one language in order to cope with the demands of daily life. Indeed, it now appears that the whole question of illiteracy at the global level is entangled with that of learning a second language since the majority of countries in the world are not monolingual, and a majority of the world's population lives in a relatively small number of very populous multilingual countries where the opportunities to become literate in the mother language are unevenly distributed among the different language groups.

It is estimated that there are over 6,000 different languages in the world, but many of them – rare flowers of human thought – are dying out. Only 12 are estimated to have around 100 million or more speakers. . . . More than half the world's languages are concentrated in only 7 countries – Papua New Guinea (850), Indonesia (670), Nigeria (410), India (380), Cameroon (270), Australia (250) and Mexico (240) . . . Another 15 countries each harbour more than 100 different languages (Zaire, Brazil, Philippines, former USSR, Malaysia, United States of America, China, Sudan, Vanuatu, Central African Republic, Myanmar and Nepal). Bilingualism is common in a majority of these countries, and for significant parts of the population in some of them literacy is only feasible in a second language because the mother language has no established orthography or written material. The gradual spread of literacy throughout the South, therefore, has required a degree of cultural flexibility and tolerance that statistics of literacy do not measure.

*Source:* UNESCO, 1993, pp. 25–27

## Efficiency considerations

All the indicators and categories listed above have an efficiency component. Efficiency describes a relationship between the costs of inputs and outputs (the desired goals and outcomes of the system). A project is efficient if it produces benefits or gains enough to justify the capital outlay. There are two concepts which need to be examined in relation to efficiency and education.

Internal efficiency of education – this is a measure of how a given investment in education improves the quality of an educational outcome. Any investment, be it remedial, teacher training or curriculum reform, should result in quality learning or improved outputs from the system. High repetition and drop out rates suggest wastage and a low internal efficiency of education.

---

### Box 7

**Hypothetical Example: Literacy Programme Costs vs Benefits**

We wish to ascertain the benefits and costs associated with three strategies for improving adult literacy:

1. Standard classroom approach with 25–30 students per teacher for 2–hour classes, three times a week;

2. Self-instruction with technological aids, for example, cassettes, programme texts and standard classes once a week;

3. Three standard classes per week as well as one remedial session with no more than 5 students.

The following table shows the hypothetical benefits in monetary terms that should accrue for each of the groups.

| Strategy | Costs | Benefits | C/B |
|----------|-----------|-----------|------|
| 1. | $200,000 | $250,000 | 0.80 |
| 2. | $150,000 | $125,000 | 1.20 |
| 3. | $350,000 | $420,000 | 0.83 |

In order to consider any particular programme, the benefits must at least be equal to the costs. Of the three, the self-instruction strategy has a cost-benefit greater than unity, meaning that costs exceed benefits.

*Source:* Adapted from Levin, 1983, pp. 22–25

---

External efficiency of education – this is a measure of how investments in the education of an individual can result in increased income or earnings to the individual.

Cost benefit and cost effectiveness analysis are ways of verifying efficiency. In cost benefit analysis an attempt is made to evaluate various alternatives or innovations by comparing their costs and benefits, measured in monetary terms.

---

**Activity 4**

- Attempt to identify the costs associated with each strategy. Costs include all the resources that are used to carry out an activity, even if they are difficult to quantify. The third strategy is the most costly. Suggest why this might be so.

- Consider how we may be able to assess benefit, i.e. literacy gains in this case, so that we can convert benefits to monetary gains, to compare costs. How may pecuniary benefits accrue to an individual from improved literacy?

---

Cost effectiveness, on the other hand, has certain outcomes or goals in mind, and will evaluate different alternatives along two measures – their costs and their effects in producing the targeted outcomes or goals. The innovation to be adopted would be the one that can produce the desired outcomes at a competitive price.

## Box 8

### Table 3.2. Hypothetical Example: Remedial Maths Programme: Costs vs Effectiveness

The table below summarises costs and effectiveness data for four remedial maths programmes that are being considered. To obtain data on effectiveness there must be a control group where no treatment is being given so as to compare achievement (or effectiveness) amongst the different groups.

| Method | Cost per student | Effectiveness (test score) | C/E |
|---|---|---|---|
| 1. Small groups working with a special tutor | $300 | 20 | $15 |
| 2. IPI – individually programmed instruction in which the student works at his own pace in a special resource room with individualised materials and co-ordinator | $100 | 4 | $25 |
| 3. CAI – computer aided instruction, includes a 10-minute session of drill and practice in arithmetic concepts, problems and operations | $150 | 15 | $10 |
| | $50 | 10 | $5 |
| 4. Peer tutoring in which older students spend 30 minutes a day tutoring those needing remediation | | | |

*Source:* Adapted from Levin, 1983, pp.19–21

## Activity 5

- *Suggest the items in each method that contribute to the costs shown.*

- *Which approach is the most effective as determined by test scores?*

- *Which approach is most cost-effective?*

- *What is the important point here for those who have to finance the system?*

- *For a context that you describe, explain which of these methods or combination of methods you would choose.*

- *It is said of this method that it does not allow the planner to make an overall determination of whether a programme is worthwhile in the sense that its benefits exceed its costs. What does this mean?*

Both cost benefit and cost effectiveness analyses are valuable tools for those concerned with financing the education system as efficiently as possible. Boxes 9 and 10 provide evidence relevant to assessments of the internal efficiency of the education system. Activities 6,7, and 8 examine various aspects of the internal efficiency of education.

---

**Box 9**

**Table 3.3. Internal Efficiency at the First Level of Education in Selected Countries (1990)**

| Country | Percentage of repeaters | Percentage of the 1989 cohort reaching | | | Coefficient of efficiency |
|---|---|---|---|---|---|
| | | Grade 2 | Grade 4 | Final grade | |
| Burundi | 22 | 89 | 77 | 77 | 0.70 |
| Lesotho | 22 | 85 | 73 | 50 | 0.54 |
| Haiti | 13 | 80 | 55 | 39 | 0.53 |
| Trinidad & Tobago | 3 | 100 | 89 | 89 | 0.92 |
| India | 4 | 92 | 68 | 62 | 0.74 |
| Denmark | 0 | 99 | 99 | 99 | 1.00 |
| Switzerland | 2 | 100 | 100 | 100 | 1.00 |
| Tonga | 4 | 100 | 93 | 92 | 0.90 |
| New Zealand | 3 | 99 | 97 | 97 | 0.96 |

*Source:* UNESCO, 1993, pp.132–35

---

**Activity 6**

- *The table is actually charting two indicators contributing to internal efficiency in education.*
  *What are they?*
  *What implications are there for the financing of education?*

- *Which countries are maximally efficient at the primary level of education? What are the factors that probably contribute to this?*

- *Consider your own country –*
  *(a) What is the coefficient of efficiency where primary education is concerned?*
  *(b) What are the likely factors responsible for this level of efficiency?*
  *(c) Are there equity considerations in the way the two indicators seem to be distributed among different social groups and different types of schools?*

## Activity 7

### Enrolment in and costs of different curriculum areas

*These indicators allow the planner to fine-tune the financing of the system.*

- *Collect statistical data for your country for the last 5 years on enrolments and relative costs of different curricular areas at secondary school.*

- *Examine this data to determine if there are trends that have resulted in inefficiencies, i.e. curricula which may be too costly given enrolments or other factors.*

- *Consider whether there may be equity considerations in how enrolments are distributed among the different curriculum areas at secondary level.*

- *Justify recommendations for adequate levels of financing to maintain and improve the education system.*

## Box 10

### Table 3.4. Proportion of Caribbean Secondary Students Gaining 5+ Passes in CXC* (1990)

| Territory | Nos gaining 5+ passes | Total entry | Percentage gaining 5+ passes by country |
|---|---|---|---|
| Anguilla | 5 | 90 | 5.6 |
| Antigua/Barbuda | 59 | 728 | 8.1 |
| Barbados | 386 | 5,184 | 7.4 |
| Belize | 49 | 1,482 | 3.3 |
| British Virgin Is. | 4 | 168 | 2.4 |
| Dominica | 56 | 780 | 7.2 |
| Grenada | 46 | 1,401 | 3.3 |
| Guyana | 182 | 6,210 | 2.9 |
| Jamaica | 1,228 | 22,229 | 5.5 |
| Montserrat | 16 | 152 | 10.5 |
| St Kitts-Nevis | 53 | 548 | 9.7 |
| St Lucia | 189 | 1,607 | 11.8 |
| St Vincent | 81 | 1,423 | 5.7 |
| Trinidad & Tobago | 2,555 | 27,694 | 9.2 |
| Turks & Caicos | 3 | 146 | 2.1 |
| Total | 4,912 | 69,842 | 7.0 |

*Caribbean Examinations Council
Source: World Bank, 1993, p. 251

## Summary

To determine whether the education system is being adequately financed requires an in-depth knowledge of both the economics of education, as well as the factors that result in good pedagogy. Indicators such as student enrolment, teacher supply, demographic factors, equity and efficiency all represent areas of concern where there is a continual struggle to balance economies with quality teaching and learning. These indicators provide a wide range of information on which planners can exercise judgements about which aspects are being adequately financed and which are not. If quality education cannot be delivered at present levels of financing, then we must examine how we actually raise the funds to see if we can increase financing and quality at the same time.

# SECTION 2

## Overview

Modules 1 and 2, as well as Section 1 of this module, consistently portray education as being in a beleaguered position. It appears to be hemmed in by severe financial constraints, especially in regard to structural adjustment policies and very high recurrent costs. At the same time, the populations in developing countries continue to make heavy social demands on the education system – to expand provision, to increase access, to improve quality and to promote efficiency.

Even amidst the failed experiments, such as those in specialised technical-vocational training, the swelling of the ranks of the educated unemployed, and high wastage and repetition rates, both governments and private citizens remain convinced that education is a valuable and necessary asset in the improvement of the quality of life both nationally and personally. Given these factors, the question that policy makers in education and finance should be addressing is – **are we really raising the money in the best way?** In other words, if we can rethink how we source and allocate funding for the system, it is possible that we can come up with ways that may promote cost recovery and cost sharing and still maintain equity, efficiency and quality. Section 2 of this chapter closely examines the case for diversification in the financing of different levels of education.

## Objectives

At the end of Section 2, the participants should be able to:

1. Distinguish between the social and private rates of return to education;

2. Identify methods to distribute the costs of education more equitably;

3. Justify recommendations of cost sharing in educational investments;

4. Evaluate the possibilities and limitations of educational financing alternatives.

The case for sharing the burdens of educational costs rests on empirical evidence that the benefits that accrue from education are greater for the private citizen than for the state, which usually finances the education in the first place.

---

**Box 11**

**Private and Social Rates of Return to Education**

The private rate of return is consistently higher than the social rate of return. The private returns to primary education are by and large well in excess of 15 per cent, and may be as high as 50 per cent. In the case of secondary and higher education, estimates of private rates of return are also high, usually well in excess of 10 to 12 per cent, and often as high as 30 to 40 per cent.

Thus, for the individual student or family, education is usually a highly profitable personal investment. The expected benefits more than compensate for the burden of high costs, including earnings foregone. The fact that the social rate of return is always lower than the private rate of return indicates that education is highly subsidised and that the extra taxes paid by the educated do not compensate for this subsidy.

*Source:* Psacharopoulos and Woodhall, 1985, p. 117

---

## Activity 9

*Which of the following indicators refer to (a) social rates of return to education and (b) private rates of return to education:*

- *increased labour productivity;*
- *reduced birth rate;*
- *environmentally sustainable economic activities;*
- *increased earnings?*

*Investigate at least one method by which social and private rates of return are calculated.*

*The private rates of return to secondary and tertiary education are less than that to primary education. Suggest reasons why this does not discourage enrolments in secondary and tertiary education.*

*Since the private rates of return are much higher than the social rate of return, what alternatives can you suggest to distribute the burden of costs on those who benefit the most?*

*Developing countries have begun to experiment with different methods of cost recovery and cost sharing, but to date much of this effort has been in tertiary education.*

- *Suggest reasons why the state has been more ready to cut back its direct involvement in the financing of tertiary education than in that of primary or secondary education?*

- *Of the 6 potential sources of revenue listed below, which are the ones more likely to be targeted to contribute to tertiary financing, or to increase their contribution: parents, students, taxpayers, tertiary educational institutions, business partnerships, community based organisations?*

- *Can you suggest any other form of income generation that will help to share costs in tertiary education?*

Box 12 lists some of the more widespread innovations being undertaken at the tertiary level as cost recovery and financial diversification measures in both developed and developing countries.

**Box 12**

**Examples of Financial Diversification**

- an increase in the share of costs borne by students and their families
- increased reliance on loans as a form of student support, in conjunction with or instead of grants
- fees for short courses of 'continuing' or 'recurrent' education, usually at full cost
- employer sponsorship of students or trainees
- endowments of institutions, staff or halls of residence by industry, commerce or philanthropists
- research grants and contract from research councils, government departments and industry and commerce
- consultancy and sale of educational and research services
- sale of other goods and services, for example revenues from conferences and vacation lettings of student accommodation, hiring of equipment and laboratories, science, parks etc.
- gifts and endowments by alumni
- the establishment and growth of private institutions of higher education.

*Source:* Adapted from Woodhall, 1994, pp. 4–5

---

**Activity 10**

1. *Why have governments been so directly involved in bearing the costs of tertiary education in developing countries in the past?*

2. *How may questions of equity, efficiency and quality be affected by a greater cost sharing with the private sector?*

3. *Examine any institution of higher learning in your country to determine what cost recovery or financial diversification alternatives are being considered or have been put in place?*

4. *Loans are deferred payments that are advantageous to the lower income student. In the past, governments have not been able to recover much of this subsidy. What factors have prevented the smooth working of this scheme? How can it be re-organised and be made more efficient?*

5. *Reforms in education are described as competitive, finance or equity driven. How would you ensure that finance driven reforms continue to uphold equity?*

The diversification of educational financing is much less apparent at the secondary level, and even less so at the primary level. The growth of private secondary schools, especially those run by religious boards, the links forged with community-based organisations and parent-teacher efforts at fundraising are some of the ways in which financing of secondary education is being gradually diversified.

One of the most comprehensive measures to be suggested is a change in the educational management of secondary schools, i.e. the policy option of decentralisation. In the interests of efficiency it is felt that decision-making, especially about use of resources, should be located closer to schools.

---

**Box 13**

**Secondary Schools and Decentralisation**

While there are merits to the option of decentralising educational services, it is important to recognise that the options cover a range of shades from black to white. The centralist tradition includes the education systems of the Prussian state, reflected in the current German system, France and Japan. The two best examples of the decentralised tradition are the education systems of the United Kingdom and the United States.

Recent reviews of decentralisation policies argue for the need to differentiate between macro and micro levels of analysis of decentralisation: 'confusion between these two levels is what accounts for the irony of the two most decentralised educational prototypes, the US and the UK, advancing on the one hand towards greater centralisation of their systems with a renewed emphasis on national standards, a national curriculum and national testing, in the name of efficiency, whilst on the other hand experiencing strong decentralising and privatising pressures, namely in the choice movement and its offshoots. There is a lesson for the Third World in the difference between the two levels and the requirements of efficiency'. Cummings and Riddell, 1992, p. 45

*Source:* Reimers and Tiburcio, 1993, pp. 63–34.

---

## Activity 12

1. What is the 'choice' movement? How is it related to diversification of educational financing?

2. What implications are there for equity in a decentralised system?

3. If there is a role for the Ministry of Education in decentralisation, what aspects of governance do you believe can be successfully decentralised?

4. What roles do you see teachers, principals and school supervisors playing in a decentralised system?

5. The central focus in the decentralisation of schools is to improve efficiency through school autonomy. What implications are there for the diversification of educational financing?

Primary education, on the other hand, has been least affected by debates and reforms in the public financing of education.

## Activity 13

• Given that in many developing countries UPE has still not been achieved, why is there a reluctance to shift the financing of the system to the private sector?

• Investigate the nature of provision and access to Early Childhood Care and Education in your country. How does it compare with primary education? How is early childhood education financed? Can you account for the differences between the financing of early childhood and primary education?

## Summary

In Section 1, we examined the performance of the education system through indicators or descriptors which identified important information about flows, distributions and stocks in the system. In turn, these gave clues about equity and efficiency in education. If the latter are two primary goals of the education system, then the financing of the system must be organised to support those goals. Hence, to the policy makers in education and finance, indicators are vital in giving an overall picture of how the system is working. In times of financial stringency it is especially important that policy makers and planners are vigilant in ensuring that the system is being financed adequately and appropriately.

In Section 2 the issue of the diversification of educational financing was raised. The continuing high social demand for education within a context of structural adjustment has forced governments to admit their limitations in financing primary, secondary and tertiary education solely from public funds. There is now a move underway to ensure that those who benefit the most from education, especially tertiary education, are made to pay more of its costs. In addition, institutions of higher learning are exploring many avenues to earn additional funding. While such innovations are slow to make an appearance in secondary and primary education, it is inevitable that private financing will make a greater contribution to these levels of the system before long. The question always remains whether these changes in the financing of education will result in greater chances of equity, efficiency and quality in education.

---

**Activity 14**

**Wrap-up: discussion and extended reflection**

*Now that you have completed the module:*

1. *Attempt to draw up a list of the pros and cons of cost recovery measures;*

2. *Examine and comment on the issues inherent in the extract in Box 14.*

---

**Box 14**

**Equity and Educational Financing – Building National Commitment to Equity**

Many developing countries must strengthen their national commitment to distributing central government funds through a system that explicitly favours schools in disadvantaged communities. Many countries allocate national funds for primary schools equally on a per capita basis, without taking into account differences in community needs and resources. The systems in other countries demonstrate perverse biases. For example, in some countries the allocations per student are lower in rural areas, particularly in poor regions, than in urban areas. Even within cities some districts (such as slums) are grossly disadvantaged.

The national government obviously plays a central role in reducing educational inequality. In some countries that are taking greater advantage of local financing, it should help keep inequality from worsening, and in countries with highly decentralised educational systems, it should encourage equity. Solving the equity problem requires reducing or eliminating the advantage associated with a higher tax base. In effect, this means redistributing tax money in one form or another from high- to low- income communities. That task, which is not an easy one, requires consensus building and can only be undertaken by the national government. Consequently, the national government must commit itself to developing and implementing an adequate system of resource allocation that is consistent with the national definition of equity. A vigorous campaign to mobilise local resources means that the central government must play a stronger role in redistributing the resources that finance education.

*Source:* Lockheed, M and Verspoor, A, 1991, p. 202

## Suggested reading

Atkinson, G B (1983). *The Economics of Education*. London: Hodder and Stoughton.

Coombs, P and Hallak, J (1987). *Cost Analysis in Education: Tools for Policy and Planning*. Washington DC: World Bank.

Levin, H (1983). *Cost effectiveness: a primer*. Beverly Hills: Sage.

Lewin, K (1994). 'Cost recovery and the role of the state'. Paper produced for the 12th Conference of Commonwealth Ministers of Education, Pakistan.

Lockheed, M, Verspoor, A and Associates (1991). *Improving Primary Education in Developing Countries*. UK: Oxford University Press.

Ministry of Education (1994). White Paper on Educational Reform. Trinidad and Tobago.

Psacharopoulos, G and Woodhall, M (1986). *Education for Development: An Analysis of Investment Choices*. Washington DC: World Bank.

Reimers, F and Tiburcio, L (1993). *Education, Adjustment and Reconstruction: Options for Change*. Paris: UNESCO.

Woodhall, M (1994). *Financing Education: Issues and International Experience*. Paris: IIEP, UNESCO.

World Bank (1993). *Caribbean Region: Access Quality and Efficiency in Education*. Washington DC: World Bank.

UNESCO (1993). *World Education Report*. Paris: UNESCO.

# MODULE 4
# Budgeting and negotiating

## Overview

The budgetary process underlies most, if not all, aspects of the government of a country. Planners and policy makers in Ministries of Education must therefore be thoroughly conversant with the procedures associated with national budgeting so that they can make a better case in claiming resources from the central government. This module provides an insight into the budgetary process, especially the thinking underlying the formulation of sectoral and national budgets.

Objectives – the participant should be able to:

1. Distinguish between business budgets and budgets of national governments;

2. Trace the evolution of the budget process in the Commonwealth;

3. Identify the different approaches to drawing up a budget;

4. Explain the justifications made about allocations in the national budget;

5. Outline the criteria necessary for investment in education;

6. Calculate unit costs as part of the budgetary process;

7. Improve negotiating skills as part of the budgetary process.

## What is a budget?

A budget is a document which outlines in a systematic way the incomes and expenditures of an individual, a firm or a national government, for a given period of time. Usually it is drawn up as a *forecast* of the expected income and proposed spending patterns that are likely to occur during the specified period. To draw up a budget, it is considered almost mandatory that the performance of the previous budget be considered. This certainly helps in drawing up a budget that reflects as accurately as possible up-to-date income and expenditure trends. In effect then, the budget becomes a plan on which to model the financial affairs of an individual, a firm or the national economy in the short term – usually about one year.

Unlike in the case of individuals or even national governments, in business there is a strong direct relationship between income and expenditure. Firms spend money to make money. Hence, expenditure is only undertaken for the purpose of generating income. National governments, on the other hand, are not profit-seeking organisations. Their revenues and expenditures are independent. Governments develop revenue budgets from their estimation of how much income they will collect through taxes, customs and excise duties, loans and other devices. Based on this, they develop expenditure budgets in accordance with the major projects, plans and philosophy of the government in power. 'Balancing' the budget is a similar concern, albeit at different scales, to that of personal and national budgeting.

## What is the 'Appropriations Bill?'

The bid by public servants to spend government revenues in various ways has to be approved by legislative bodies. Every year the Finance Ministries of central governments present their revenue and expenditure budgets as an Appropriations Bill to Parliament for scrutiny and debate. The Appropriations Bill establishes fixed dollar amounts for various ministries and projects to achieve the objectives of government for that year. When it is passed, authorisation is obtained to spend taxpayers' money for the public good.

Like those of an individual, government's revenues are on the whole limited and fixed for selected periods. Like a monthly paycheck, taxes or customs duties cannot be increased in the short term to comply with any increasing need by the government for more money. Hence, it is absolutely necessary that assiduous care and attention be given in forecasting revenues realistically, otherwise the 'balance' of the budget may be compromised and deficits may occur.

The 'Budget', then, is the fundamental organising framework for the national government. Once the budget had passed into law, its integrity is guaranteed by various controls and mechanisms. For example, the *power of virement*, i.e. the right to move funds from an item to which it has been assigned to another item, can only be given by an Act of Parliament. Most importantly, the success of a budget (often in hindsight) is a particularly powerful comment on the ability of the government to manage the affairs of the country. Factors such as the stewardship function of government, the 'fixed' nature of revenues and the political implications of both make the national budget the most important single act of government in any year.

## Historical development of 'the budget'

Commonwealth countries have inherited a legacy of governance structures which include the cycles and procedures surrounding the formulation of annual budgets. The specific names of the various ministries and governmental bodies may differ but the basic functioning of the system remains remarkably similar, especially in the smaller Commonwealth countries. Box 1 outlines the antecedents of the 'budget' in the United Kingdom. While it illustrates the simplicity with which the budget was conceived, there are certain trends which hint at how important this device was to become in the national economy.

---

**Box 1**

**The Historical Development of the 'Budget'**

Until the time of James II (1685–8), the actual business of government was carried on directly by the King, and the expenses were met partly from his hereditary revenues (for example from Crown lands) and partly from certain taxes (for example customs duties) which Parliament voted to him for life at the beginning of each reign. If expenditure looked like becoming too great to be met from these sources, the King would ask Parliament to vote him an additional 'supply'; having done so, Parliament would then consider the 'ways and means' of raising the money, and would impose such taxes as were necessary for the purpose. It is in accordance with this ancient usage that the House of Commons still sits as 'Committee of Supply' when it debates the government's spending plans, i.e. the 'Supply Estimates', and as 'Committee of Ways and Means' when it discusses tax proposals. Since the King's needs for additional supply arose at irregular intervals, while the ordinary business of government was regarded as his own affair rather than Parliament's, there was no occasion for regular annual budgets; indeed, the word 'Budget' was not used in anything like its modern sense until 1733.[1]

After the Revolution of 1688, and still more after the accession of George I in 1714, the political predominance of Parliament led it to exert closer financial control over the administration. Most of the cost of civil government was still met from the King's life revenues (the 'Civil List', as it was called), but from 1689 onwards the country was involved in a long series of wars with France, which caused military expenditure to rise greatly; this required annual votes of supply and the annual imposition of taxes, so that it soon became customary for ministers to draw up statements of the year's revenue and expenditure for submission to Parliament. Wars were financed by borrowing as well as taxation; the

---

National Debt, beginning in 1694 at 1.2 million pounds, had grown to 213 million pounds by 1783, and the interest on it became a major item in government's outgoings. To repay the debt meant running a surplus of revenue over expenditure, while to incur a wartime deficit meant obtaining Parliamentary authority for additional borrowing; in either case, a budgetary statement was necessary to explain and justify the government's financial programme. By the time of the younger Pitt (Prime Minister from 1783 to 1801, and again from 1804 to 1806) the Budget had become well established as a part of the routine of Parliament.

Pitt introduced the principle of the 'Consolidated Fund' – that is, of having a single central account into which all receipts are paid and from which all expenditure is met. Before then, several departments had been directly receiving the proceeds of taxes which were 'earmarked' for them, and had made their own arrangements for disbursements – a system which made it difficult to impose any kind of central control, as well as creating many opportunities for the misuse of funds by ministers and officials. With all expenditure being made from the Consolidated Fund, it is relatively easy to ensure that nothing is done which has not been authorised by Parliament; with all revenue going into the Fund, no individual department can finance activities of its own which have not been so authorised; and the state of the government's revenue and expenditure as a whole can easily be calculated by comparing inflows with outflows from the Fund over any given week, month or year.

Other measures of Pitt's foreshadowed the system which emerged from Gladstone's reforms of the 1860s, whereby the year's tax changes are embodied in a single Finance Act, while the programme of government's spending is embodied in a single Appropriation Act bringing all departments' estimates together.

*Source:* Open University, 1972, pp. 38–39

[1]An anonymous pamphlet in that year compared the Chancellor (Walpole, who was also Prime Minister) to a cheapjack opening his 'budget' (or bag) of tricks. The term caught on, but lost its satirical overtone.

## Activity 1

*Box 1 shows how the budget began to take on more than just its original bookkeeping function. What aspects of the budget can you see growing in importance over time? What similarities do you discern between the historical development of the 'Budget' and its various mechanisms in the United Kingdom and your own country?*

Box 2 below gives a contemporary description of the expanded role budgets now play in national economies. In it we see the importance and care given to the processes by which the budget is drawn up. You may see a strong link between these processes and the 'aspects of the budget' that you detected in Activity 1.

---

### Box 2

**A Contemporary View of the National Budget**

Governments allocate scarce resources to programmes and services through the budget process. As a result, it is one of the most important activities undertaken by governments. As the focal point for key resource decisions, the budget process is a powerful tool. The quality of decisions resulting from the budget process and the level of their acceptance depends on the characteristics of the budget process that is used.

The budget process consists of activities that encompass the development, implementation, and evaluation of a plan for the provision of services and capital assets. A good budget is far more than the preparation of a legal document that appropriates funds for a series of line items. Good budgeting is a broadly defined process that has political, managerial, planning, communication and financial dimensions.

A good budget process is characterised by several essential features. A good budget process:

- incorporates a long-term perspective

- establishes linkages to broad organisational goals

- focuses budget decisions on results and outcomes

- involves and promotes effective communication with stakeholders

- provides incentives to government, management and employees.

These key characteristics of good budgeting make clear that the budget process is not simply an exercise in balancing revenues and expenditures one year at a time, but is strategic in nature, encompassing a multi-year financial and operating plan that allocates resources on the basis of identified goals. A good budget process moves beyond the traditional concept of line item expenditure control, providing incentives and flexibility to managers that can lead to improved program efficiency and effectiveness.

*Source:* National Advisory Council on State and Local Budgeting, 1997

Budgets then, have undergone evolution and metamorphosis, so much
so that they are often now used as a means to judge whether a government
is competent in handling its affairs. This evaluation rests on the fact that the
ways of drawing up budgets (see Box 3) have evolved into very
sophisticated procedures that allow for greater control of resources,
greater accountability in the disbursement and use of those resources, and
a better understanding of the budget as a tool which can be used to effect
the plans and programmes of a government for the common good. In
essence then, this expanded notion of good budgeting amounts to good
government.

---

**Table 4.1. Ministry of Education – Estimate of the Amount Required in
the year ending 31 December 1996 for the Salaries and Expenses of the
Ministry (\*$1,179,627,224)**

(Sub-heads under which this vote will be accounted for by the Ministry)

| Sub-heads | 1994 actual | 1995 estimates | 1995 rev. estimate | 1996 estimates | Variance |
|---|---|---|---|---|---|
| Personnel | 699,566,336 | 773,095,642 | 730,365,000 | 784,320,000 | 53,955,000 |
| Goods & services | 79,005,794 | 90,202,944 | 99,970,000 | 110,149,772 | 10,179,772 |
| Minor equipment | 436,522 | 680,000 | 680,000 | 1,000,000 | 320,000 |
| Current transfers & subsidies | 132,471,139 | 149,417,671 | 150,036,800 | 158,827,172 | 8,790,372 |
| Current transfers to statutory boards | 240,013 | 336,420 | 352,620 | 230,280 | 122,340 |
| Total recurrent expenditure | 911,719,804 | 1,013,732,677 | 981,404,420 | 1,054,527,224 | 73,122,804 |
| Capital development programme | 94,202,957 | 99,430,000 | 132,177,000 | 125,100,000 | 7,077,000 |
| Total head | 1,005,922,761 | 1,113,162,677 | 1,113,581,420 | 1,179,627,224 | 66,045, 804 |

*Source:* Republic of Trinidad & Tobago, 1995, p.132.
\*$=T&T

## Box 3

### Approaches to Budgeting

**Line Item Budgeting** – This technique has been widely used for many years in assigning amounts to each expenditure category of the budget. In line item budgeting, the emphasis is placed on the specific *objects* for which funds are expended wherein each line item shown in the budget document is assumed to be the proper base for an expenditure. As a result, budgets are planned around each line item separately, and the new budget is based on increases applied to each line's base – usually the expenditure level of the previous budget cycle – see Table 4.1 opposite.

The major benefit of line item budgeting is that the budget is considered to be the sum of its parts, with each part considered separately in terms of some measure of need. Further, it permits some tracking of expenditures over time. Finally, it suggests some consideration of programmatic needs, although the concept is not as sophisticated as other techniques discussed below. Because it has been in place for many years and because it is easily understood, it has survived despite the advent of other more sophisticated budgeting techniques.

Despite historic popularity, there are several drawbacks to line item budgeting that deserve consideration. A major drawback is that this technique depends on the budget document almost exclusively for allocation decisions. . . . Too little information is provided about how allocations are made, the process is too dependent on experience, and little or no record of decision processes is evident.

Obviously, the use of such a method fosters the cloistered appearance of budgets, vests decisions in only a few persons, and does not facilitate the greater degree of accountability required of today's educational planners.

**Programme (or Performance Budgeting)** – Development of programme budgeting represents movement of the budget process into a more modern phase. Also known as *functional budgeting* or *function-object budgeting,* programme budgeting differs from line item budgeting in that the various funds in a budget are internally organised according to their specific objective or purpose. The budget document no longer serves as the decision document because a more sophisticated method of fund structures is used for internal decision and control processes. Enabling this process is an elaborate system, developed with the advent of electronic accounting systems using various national reporting standards, wherein sub-accounts break expenditures in a budget into incrementally smaller parts related to how the money is used.

*Source:* Adapted from Thompson, Wood and Honeyman, 1994, pp.309–10

In many Commonwealth countries, the central financing unit uses a system of line item budgeting while the various ministries use programme budgeting. In most cases a hybrid system emerges where there is the traditional line item classification but it is expanded to incorporate a breakdown of activities or projects associated with each line item. However, there is a perceived need on the part of planners in the system to move closer to the demands and thus the benefits of programme budgeting.

The requirements of programme budgeting are:

- a high level of intra-governmental coordination between the administrative agencies responsible for budgeting matters and overall development planning, for example preparation of annual budgets within the context of the longer-range planning framework of the national development plan;

- setting both short-term and long-term goals and objectives;

- formulating specific programmes and related projects in terms of the set goals and objectives;

- setting performance targets in relation to the programmes and projects and linked to the overall goals and objectives;

- internal restructuring of government ministries and departments to implant the required skills and the management structures to carry out the envisaged tasks;

- cost accounting methodologies compared with the cash-based accounting associated with line item budgeting;

- expertise in accurate calculation of unit costs.

Some of the benefits of programme budgeting are:

- greater control and accountability;

- inter-agency co-operation of the planning and budgeting function, as well as co-ordination between the Ministries of Finance and the spending ministries;

- an assessment of tasks and activities accomplished in the budget period;

- an assessment of the cost-effectiveness of the specific tasks that were approved to be performed in the budget period.

*Source:* Adapted from Commonwealth Secretariat, 1997

## Box 4

### Programme, Planning and Budgeting Systems (PPBS)

Given the progress represented by programme budgeting, the next logical step was greater refinement through a system that linked programmes, planning and budgeting into a more integrated whole. PPBS is a method for improving how decisions are made about the allocation of scarce resources. For example, suppose instruction in schools needed to be improved. This goal will be tied into every step and level between the chalkface and the national planning system. Along the way alternative methods of improving instruction will be considered in terms of costs and benefits. PPBS is a means of organising information so that the consequences of particular choices can be seen clearly.

This system revolutionises how budgets are conceptualised. It requires that each ministry, and each level within a ministry (and that includes each school) systematically formulate their own developmental plans in broad agreement with national goals. Programmes of spending are then earmarked based on perceived needs and goals. The same desired outcomes are reflected in all the linked plans from the national to the individual school level. A clear relationship is thus evident of what outcomes or objectives were funded and an evaluation made as to the benefits of such expenditure.

The recent thrust towards decentralisation of schools and the need to implement school based management procedures highlights the importance of this approach to budgeting. PPBS contributes powerfully to the concept of accountability, both as a consequence of its focus on outcomes and by its ability to continue and extend the object-function code account system to include analysis of success. For example, at the level of the school a major function code such as 'buildings and classrooms' can be broken down to the outcomes stated by an individual teacher of an expenditure that would be tracked by account code and linked to some assessment criteria such as standardised test scores.

*Source:* Adapted from Thompson, Wood and Honeyman, 1994, pp.310–11

## Activity 2

- *What approaches to budgeting are evident in your country at the national and ministerial levels?*

- *What strategies and mechanisms do you foresee as necessary for the proper implementation of a programme budgeting system at both levels?*

Box 4 goes on to describe a more sophisticated budget design known as Programme, Planning and Budgeting Systems.

This model of budgeting is conceptually quite advanced and requires sophisticated know-how to implement, especially in regard to the accumulation of its database and the use of systematic accounting procedures. Many countries have been stymied in their desire to implement this system by the inherent complexities. The Cook Islands use this type of budgeting, called 'output budgeting', at both the national and ministerial levels. The following is an example of how they organise one output for budgeting purposes.

---

**Box 5**

**The Curriculum – Performance Indicators**

| Deliverables | Measures | Qualitative Indicators |
|---|---|---|
| Implementation of the Primary School Science Curriculum by the Secretary of Education | Quality of syllabus to meet standard required by the Secretary of Education | Syllabus endorsed by the Secretary of Education and implementation by 30 June 1998. |

---

From the above we get the picture that this form of budgeting goes far beyond the juggling of funds. Allocations are based on making the programmes in which those funds will be expended explicit, and furthermore, criteria, timelines and measurement and evaluation are applied at various stages before more funds can be accessed.

---

**Activity 3**

- *Consider the implications of implementing PPBS in a country with which you are familiar. How will the budgeting process need to be conceptualised in order to fulfil the requirements of PPBS?*

- *PPBS is sometimes described as having a different value system to that of other budgeting systems. One way in which this has been understood is that there are thought to be potential conflicts between programmes and staff for scarce resources. Suggest a relevant example.*

- *PPBS is also understood as forcing a climate of accountability in social and political structures which have been historically non-accountable. How far do you agree with this description?*

The approach to budgeting known as zero-based budgeting (Box 6) has become more relevant to countries struggling with structural adjustment imperatives in an era of financial stringency. The overall philosophy of this budgetary approach has to do with cost-cutting and is economical in its emphasis, rather than discriminatory, where equity and pedagogical issues are concerned. It reflects the tension that is always present in educational financing – to what extent can we maintain considerations of equity, efficiency and quality education in our decisions about financing the system.

## Box 6

### Zero-Based Budgeting

Zero-based budgeting is an example of how external political realities can press changes on educational organisations during an era of fiscal austerity and retrenchment. Often thought to be a military concept, ZBB was first instituted in the federal government under President Carter as an effort to trim federal spending through implementation of sunset laws designed to zero out unproductive or unjustified government programmes. . . . Broadly appealing psychologically, the basic premise supporting ZBB is that all budget categories must be completely re-justified each fiscal year to cut waste and thus improve organisational and fiscal efficiency. From an operational perspective, all budget categories must be set at zero and those responsible for preparing budgets must carefully justify the amount of money to be placed in each fund. To complete each budget cycle requires rebuilding the need for every staff position, every piece of new equipment, and every supply purchased.

The conceptual benefits of ZBB are obvious. The product of an era of high inflation and discontent with government waste, ZBB represented a better chance of assuaging taxpayer anger by giving the impression of strong government action to reduce both waste and government growth. Additionally, the concept had other legitimate bases, particularly that budget growth should not continue unchecked without serious questions about positive contribution to the educational enterprise.

Despite ZBB's conceptual strength, many problems were experienced in its operationalisation. Like PPBS, the process of zeroing budgets was extremely complicated for a variety of important reasons. ZBB was also often criticised as a cost reduction method that required more resources for effective preparation than could be saved by the process. The same problems of internal strife seen in PPBS were also inherent to zero-based budgeting, as elective and enrichment courses were indiscriminately asked to exhibit the same justification for existence as core areas of instruction. Additionally, the notion of zeroing core courses was inherently impossible creating incredulity. Although most persons would likely describe ZBB as a fundamentally good idea, its problems were so significant that many districts have abandoned the concept in recent years. Vestiges of ZBB still linger, however, as many districts have continued the concept of preparing best case – no growth – worst case scenarios given the present uncertain revenue prospects commonly faced by schools in many states.

*Source:* Adapted from Thompson, Wood and Honeyman, 1994, pp. 312–13

---

### Activity 4

- *The approaches to budgeting described so far represent different philosophical positions of the relationships between revenues, expenditures and programmes.*

- *Reflect on the budgetary philosophy in your country and suggest what value positions are accorded each of these in drawing up the 'Budget'.*

- *Under what circumstances do you see zero-based budgeting as a valuable exercise?*

## What is the national budgetary process?

In most countries of the Commonwealth the responsibility for producing the budget is assigned to the Minister of Finance. The first step is a circular sent out to all ministries giving detailed instructions to permanent secretaries and heads of departments on the procedures to be followed in the preparation and submission of the draft estimates of expenditure for the coming year. Analysis of the present budget is a must as it informs proposals for the next budget. Box 7 below is an excerpt from such a circular.

**Box 7**

**Minister of Finance Circular No.3 dated May 13, 1997**

- 1.5 The 1998 Budget will be circumscribed by the following documents:

  - the Medium Term Policy Framework (MTPF) 1997–1999; and

  - the Strategic Plan and Draft 1998 Workplan of each Ministry, Department or Agency.

- 1.6 With respect to the MTPF the following should be noted:

  - The MTPF outlines Government's macroeconomic management programme and its sectoral development policies over the next three years. The MTPF also presents projections of key macro-economic indicators including the GDP growth rate, the fiscal balance, the balance of payments and external financing requirements for the period.

  - Over the last three years, Trinidad and Tobago returned to the path of economic growth, and this trend is expected to continue over the medium term. To realise the desired level of economic development, Government must continue to meet its objectives of growth and efficiency, and at the same time deal with the challenges which emerge in achieving the social objectives of equity and poverty reduction, and the ecological objective of sound natural resource management.

  - These objectives will be met by increasing the level of investment in those sectors, where there is potential for increasing employment. The agriculture, tourism, construction and manufacturing sectors have been targeted to assist Government in its objective of poverty reduction, unemployment relief, and growth of the non-oil sector.

- Permanent Secretaries, Heads of Departments and Senior Managers are to ensure that their organisations' plans inform their budgetary proposals. Indeed, Ministries/Departments are advised to have their planning processes and activities coincide with and linked to the budgetary exercise in order to make a simple but definitive progressive step towards programme budgeting for the more effective allocation of resources.

*Source:* Republic of Trinidad & Tobago,1998, pp. 4–59

Box 7 illustrates the nature of the directives circulated to ministries as a preamble to drawing up the national budget. It is apparent that important decisions have already been made as to the areas in which the government feels funding should occur. One would expect that a preliminary stage occurred before this when each ministry would be given a chance to make a case for funding their own projects. A clear picture emerges here that ministry representatives must have a very good and well-researched case in hand when making a bid for national funds.

---

### Activity 5

*The directives of a Ministry of Finance excerpted in Box 7 give us an idea of the key philosophical assumptions about budgeting that is evident in this country at this time.*

- *Evaluate the nature of these assumptions as they concern – a specific budgetary approach, a developmental perspective for the country, linkages between broad organisational goals, justification for priority areas, and involvement of all in the process.*

- *One notion of the mission of the budget process states that:*
  *'. . . the budget process is to help decision makers make informed choices for the provision of services and capital assets and to promote stakeholder participation in the decision process'. (NACSLB, 1997)*

*What is your impression of the nature of stakeholder participation as described in Box7?*

---

Interviews undertaken with participants from Ministries of Education and Finance in Tokelau, Niue, Fiji, Samoa, Tonga, the Solomon Islands, Vanuatu and the Cook Islands resulted in the following criticisms of the budgetary process in their countries:

- little consultation between those proposing budgets and those finalising the budget;

- what the Ministry of Education thought may be important was viewed differently by those with the final say;

- unrealistic expectations by heads of departments always led to significant budget cuts;

- little or no consultation between the Ministry of Education and other ministries;

- too little time left in the budget cycle for proper screening and debate of budget proposals;

- feedback to ministries was lacking;

- little or no input from teachers and principals in the proposals coming from the Ministry of Education.

*Source:* Adapted from Commonwealth Secretariat, 1997

---

**Activity 6**

- *Consider the budget process in your country. To what extent are these criticisms applicable to your context?*

- *To your knowledge, have there been improvements in the budgetary process in any of the countries mentioned?*

- *How can the budget process be improved?*

---

Once the estimates of expenditure from the various ministries and government departments reach the Ministry of Finance, the task becomes two-fold. Firstly, on the expenditure side final decisions have to be made on the allocation of funds so as to effectively achieve the intentions of the Government and be in close accord with the wishes of the population. Justification for budgetary allocations depends on these questions:

- What purposes will be achieved by this expenditure?

- What will be the benefits and costs of spending the money in this way?

- Should more or less be allocated to a particular service?

- Can the money be spent more efficiently to achieve a given purpose?

Secondly, on the revenue side deliberations have to take into account the desire to distribute the burdens of taxation in a politically acceptable fashion. This task is solely concerned with the short-run economic effects of the budget. The thinking behind the budget is often a source of concern to citizens and officials of the various ministries. In Box 8 below a government official responsible for the final say in drawing up the budget reflects on his government's intentions.

## Box 8

### New Strategies for Formulating the Budget

This is ideally what a budget is supposed to do. But of course, we never attain the ideal and never are able to satisfy everyone in the community. If we reduce taxation, some people say that this is giving concession to the rich or to the establishment. If we increase taxation, it's supposed to be inhibiting investment and development of the industrial and agricultural sectors, etc. If we come down too heavily on industry, the agriculturalists say that we haven't given enough assistance to agriculture, etc.

I don't believe that anybody who works on a budget or who actually tries to prepare a budget is ever able to satisfy everybody in a community. I am talking now about a national budget, as opposed to a budget of say, a firm. But even in firms, you have problems between departments and division when you come to discuss the capital budget of a company.

Now I would like to spend a little time to explain how we do the budget exercise. We are involved in what is known as 'double budgeting', in a sense that you have a recurrent budget, which takes care of the recurrent expenditure of the Government, including wages, etc., and we have the capital budget which deals with the development programme. Both of these exercises involve a great deal of work – quantitative work – and especially the capital budget, and for which we depend a lot for our inputs on the ministries and the agencies of government. In order to try and get a picture of what these agencies and ministries want to do, how they want to spend the money they hope to get, we send out, very early in the year, a very comprehensive circular, in other words, the circulars contained requests for both the recurrent estimates and the capital budgetary estimates.

What we have also tried to do is not to indulge in arbitrary cutting. Previously, one of the very big problems in the budget exercise and in the implementation of the budget was that in the Ministry of Finance, because of the lack of information, or lack of coordination a lot of the cutting and the pruning in the budget exercise was done in a very arbitrary fashion. What we have tried to do is to ask the people in the ministries and the agencies to rank their projects so that we will have some indication of where they feel their priorities lie among their total project package. This is so because if we have to cut back, in cutting we use their ranking and not just cut arbitrarily and so interfere with ongoing programmes which they feel are more important than other programmes which they have included in their submission. So we have put all this in our circular and we endeavour to get back from the ministries their estimates, so that we could have comprehensive discussions with them in detail on every aspect of their programme, and pull everything together, so that we have a comprehensive picture of the way in which the money will be spent overall and what impact the expenditure will have on the economy as a whole.

Now, I am not here trying to criticise my colleagues in any way, but one of the problems which we face is that many of the ministries do not submit their estimates on time. Very few ministries in fact do this, and this creates a serious problem for the people in the Ministry of Finance. We are forced then to do the Budget Expenditure Exercise without having the kind of detailed discussion that we would like to have with the ministries concerned. Several of them do not give the kind of information we want with regard to the ranking of the project, and again, this pushes us back into a situation where we have to arbitrarily, or using our best guesses or best knowledge, cut their programmes when they require cutting from the way we see it, and not from the way we see it in collaboration with them.

When we get in all the submissions, we then try to put the budget back together and see how much we can give to each Ministry. This is where the question of the relationship between recurrent and capital expenditure also arises, because a lot of the capital expenditure which is contained in the Capital Budget has implications for the Recurrent Budget, and this is where we have to do a very careful exercise in seeing what capital programmes – what a particular capital programme will mean in terms of recurrent expenditure which will be required in the fiscal year in question.

*Source:* Barsotti, 1992, pp. 176–78

The Ministry of Finance prepares the final version of the budget to be laid in the House. Once parliamentary authorisation is obtained the budget is implemented. In the following year, the performance of the budget comes up for audit. Reports from the Auditor General's office are laid in the House and these are examined by the Public Accounts Committee.

This is the **budget cycle**. In any given year, budgets for three years – the previous year, the budget year and the following year – come under consideration. For the previous year's budget, analysis and auditing are being carried out. For the present year, the budget is being executed and monitored. For the following year, ministries and departments are in the process of preparing draft estimates.

Thus, although in principle the previous year's budget must be consulted in order to draw up this year's budget, it is often the case that this year's budget has to be implemented immediately the previous budgetary year finishes while the previous budget is still undergoing auditing and review. Hence, budgets are being developed only on a preliminary analysis of the previous budget's performance.

## What is the response of the Ministry of Education?

The concerns of Ministries of Education in Commonwealth countries should be on increasing their understanding of the national budgetary process so that they could make a more informed bid for state resources. This would focus attention internally on how the ministry goes about developing its plans and programmes, how it approaches the task of producing its draft estimates of expenditure and, how much it appreciates the dilemmas and intentions of central governments in the final allocation of resources.

At the same time, the onus is on the Ministry to educate decision makers in finance about the nature and purpose of education. This can best be done if the Ministry produces well-crafted and expertly budgeted plans that echo the national goals of the country. Negotiating skills thus come into play – first, in how budget documents are prepared, and secondly, in crucial meetings between both ministries where Education's proposals have to be justified and defended.

The development of sound budgets therefore is an essentially political undertaking. The deliberations of the planner in Box 8 seem to be largely a process of weighing up what resources exist against what is requested and then proceeding towards rational distribution. However, Box 9 suggests some political issues that are also important to Ministry of Education officials in formulating their budget proposals.

---

**Activity 8**

*While reading the excerpt in Box 9 below, consider the issues embedded in the following questions.*

- *Since Ministries of Education already have ratified plans for education over a specified period, how can they deal with variations in annual budget allocations that stray far from original estimates?*

- *Since the making of effective budgets seems to lie in the realms of politics and economics, should Education Ministries engage in economic forecasting and political analysis?*

- *Since education already receives a large slice of expenditure allocations, how can Ministry officials produce effective budget proposals requiring even more expenditure?*

- *'. . . the true genius of enlightened educational planning lies in how closely and effectively technical skills and political insights can be brought to bear upon the achievement of a given set of objectives' (Weiler, 1984, p.474). Discuss.*

## Box 9

### The Politics of Resource Allocation and Utilisation

One of the reasons why education is such an eminently conflictual, and hence political, element in virtually any society is its claim on a major portion of a country's resources and the potential for this claim to be contested by other sectors of state activity. This observation bears directly on the question of why educational plans face problems of implementation. Probably the single most important reason why educational plans that are otherwise well designed encounter problems of implementation is concerned with the availability of the right resources at the right time. Plans are always designed with certain assumptions about the kind and quantity of resources that will be available at given points over the planning period; these assumptions normally take the form of political commitments made at the time the plan was designed and reflect, in turn, political choices about priorities in a country's development policies.

These priorities, as we are aware, have a way of changing over time, sometimes over relatively short periods of time, and these changes tend to alter materially the assumptions about available resources on which a given plan was predicated in the first place. In theory, of course, plans can be changed in order to reflect changed circumstances; in reality, however, plans in education as elsewhere, tend to assume a fairly solid existence of their own once they have been made, and the adjustment to a changing resource situation is often made on an ad hoc basis at the interface between plan and implementation.

Where changes in the resource base for the implementation of educational plans can potentially be of such importance, an understanding of the factors that might lead to these changes becomes a matter of prime importance for those interested in the development of an education system. Such an understanding would include a realistic assessment of the stability and resilience of the country's overall resource base (and an understanding of the economic and political factors that might endanger that stability, such as world price fluctuation or armed conflict); a 'map' of the political weights of competing claims on that resource base, which would involve an assessment of the political strength of different ministries and other public agencies and their leadership; and a reading on the seriousness with which the country's leadership is committed to the aspirations embedded in the educational plan. It lies in the nature of things political that each of these can only be imperfectly ascertained. Nonetheless, the important task seems to be to reduce, by whatever degree seems feasible, the level of uncertainty that surrounds in many cases the resource assumptions of educational plans. My point is that such a task primarily requires a political analysis.

*Source:* Weiler, 1984, pp.472–73

Officials in the Ministry of Education can negotiate a more receptive audience for their budgetary plans and programmes, if they also consider that part of their task is to educate the decision makers in finance about the nature and purpose of education. Box 10 below illustrates the conflicting demands that economists and education planners have for increasing investment in education.

---

### Box 10

#### The Privileged Position that Education should have in the National Plan

For the economic planning experts, education has a double aspect: in the short term (the period of a 4- or 5-year plan), the economy must try to provide education with the means it requires to expand, not only because it trains future workers, but because of the other factors we have referred to. Economic expansion will not benefit during this short period from these supplementary efforts made on behalf of education; on the contrary, they will delay the entry of young men and women into the active population, and may even mean a reduction in the amount of productive investment.

In the medium or long term, as a result of earlier educational expansion plans, the active population will derive the benefit of an expanding flow of better-educated and trained young people. This will gradually transform the intellectual and vocational structure of the population. The higher skills of the active population will make it possible for production techniques to be constantly improved and for the steady progress of economic expansion. From this angle, there is no doubt that educational development is an investment. The advantages of this type of investment are not restricted to the sort economists try to calculate but are felt in all spheres, whether social, domestic, cultural or democratic.

This investment should be given a privileged position in national development plans, which not only aim at raising production and the standard of living but concern every aspect of human society. However, the financial priority which must be given to education does not in any way exclude – indeed, because of the large sums expended on education, it requires – the making of every effort to rationalise the use of such funds and to obtain the best possible returns.

*Source:* Poignant, 1967, p. 47

## Activity 9

*Outline a presentation that you would make to top officials in the Ministry of Finance about the importance, not only of maintaining the present investment in education, but of significantly increasing that investment.*

## Box 11

### The Human Factor in the Development Matrix

The concept of development underlying the notion of human competence is predicated on the role of people as autonomous participants in the process of social change and improvement, capable (competent) of both understanding the complex dynamics of development processes and of affecting and influencing the direction of these processes. Just as 'development' has many facets, the human capabilities and competencies required to participate actively in these different facets range as widely.

Once we understand development as no longer limited to the realm of economic production and consumption, but as also including such things as the sustenance of cultural traditions and identities, the quality and ease of interpersonal and intergroup communication and action, the inculcation and growth of active and critical citizenship, the possibility for recreation and leisure time, and the achievement and preservation of good health, the range of 'human competence' required to sustain this wide array of development objectives expands correspondingly. For example, it is obvious that poor health and nutrition will have a detrimental effect on a person's ability to participate in the process of economic production. At the same time, however, there is absolute and independent value in sustaining peoples' health and physical well-being regardless of its impact on their productive abilities.

The notion of human competence as a key issue in development, and the complex set of social interventions involved, present a major challenge to the world of policy. At the policy as well as at the conceptual level, some of the simplifications of conventional and overly narrow models of human resource development will have to give way to more complex and comprehensive policy strategies. These strategies will have to be cognisant of both the broader range of competencies that form the objectives of human competence development, and of the richer set of social interventions that can be mobilised to achieve those objectives.

*Source:* Adapted from Chinapah, Löfstedt and Weiler, 1989, pp. 21–23

One way that education personnel may consider in trying to persuade central authorities to release more funding for educational projects is to advocate an understanding of the educational enterprise as one encompassing all facets of social life (Box 11). In this way the project of education becomes equated with the goals of development which are also the concerns of central government .

---

### Activity 10

*Analyse a recent national budget proposal. What paradigms or perspectives are most evident about development – economical, human competence or others?*

---

Even though education can substantially justify its claim for a 'privileged' position on the national budget, it must, like all other sectoral interests, present the most economical case to the central government. This would entail:

(i)   the expert calculation of unit costs (Boxes 12 and 13) and

(ii)  the careful analysis of training priorities for investment (Box 14)

---

### Box 12

**Calculation of Unit Costs**

Cost analysis in education is typically calculated in terms of units. The unit cost of a good or service represents the ratio between the cost (of production, sale or purchase) of a given quantity of goods or services and the quantity expressed as a number of units. The valuation of the unit cost of the service of education implicitly presupposes that the production of education can be quantified. We can distinguish two ways of quantifying the production of education: (a) by reference to the number of examination successes or academic performance; and (b) by reference to attendance. Under (a), the simplest units to count are the number of examination successes, or, more generally, the number of pupils reaching a certain standard of education. Under (b), the practice is to consider either production capacity in terms of the number of teachers, classes or places, or attendance itself by reference to the number of pupil-years (or more simply of pupils) or the average daily attendance (ADA). We shall now consider the advantages and disadvantages of these different forms of unit costs.

**Cost per graduate.** The average cost per graduate (i.e. per successful candidate in the terminal examination at each level of education) is arrived at by taking a notional cohort of pupils or students, assessing the total cost of educating them until they have all quit the education sector and calculating the total number of graduates in the cohort. The average cost per graduate is the ratio of total cost to number of graduates. A much simpler method is – after estimating the average number of graduates over a period of time, and the ratio between this average and actual enrolments, calculate the total cost of education, and, consequently, the average cost per graduate. This kind of unit costing affords some valuable indications of the efficiency of education systems. The comparison of the theoretical costs and the real costs indicates the volume of economic wastage from dropout and repeating. However, assigning the whole financial burden to graduates alone has the effect of substantially increasing the cost per graduate, since it disregards the other pupils who quit the education system after attaining a certain level.

**Cost by level of education attained.** For this reason, not only graduates but pupils who quit the system after completing one, two, three, etc., years of study, should be included. This is a more precise costing procedure as those who quit the system before graduating have nevertheless acquired some education and knowledge, which is appreciated, in particular, by their prospective employers. It is therefore only fitting that they should be taken into account in costing.

Unit cost per pupil. This is the formula most currently used. It is the ratio between recurrent money costs and enrolments; recurrent costs only and not capital costs are taken, since the ratio between capital expenditure in any given year and the number of enrolments in that year would have little significance.

**Cost per average daily attendance.** In some countries, and to allow for the fact that the number of enrolments does not always match the actual attendance, another formula has been adopted, namely that of dividing recurrent costs by a magnitude representing the number of pupils attending each day, i.e. the 'average daily attendance'. Thus, Canada and the United States of America, for example, publish for primary and secondary education costs by average daily attendance.

**Capital cost per class.** For capital expenditure, it is significant to use the formula of cost per place by relating the cost of construction and initial equipment to the number of places provided. This cost is very useful in making projections. The techniques habitually used in the choice of investments can easily be applied to school building by comparing the annual cost per place of different projects, the costs being estimated in the light of the economic life of the different projects and the appropriate cash flow discount rate.

**The Educational Price Index** – Unit cost projections are made at a general level of constant prices. Each of the goods and services which enters into the production of education has its individual price trend, with the result that the average price index of the service of education varies even at the general level of constant prices; unit costs must therefore be adjusted in the light of this trend. The indexes which reflect these variations are usually called 'relative price indexes'.

*Source:* Adapted from Hallak, 1969, pp. 41–43 and 52

## Activity 11

- *How can unit costs be used by decision makers to assess the internal and external performance of education?*

- *As far as you know, what information is available to Ministry of Education officials to help them in the calculation of unit costs?*

- *Investigate how educational price indices are constructed for a selected country.*

- *Interview a policy maker or planner in the Ministry of Education in a country with which you are familiar. To what extent is there an emphasis on the calculation of unit costs to support decisions about educational programmes?*

## Box 13

### Unit Costs and Curriculum Decision Making

The unit costs of academic education and vocational education at the secondary level have been the subject of many economic analyses, often fueled by the long-standing debate over the relative merits of two types of curriculum to meet the employment and manpower needs of a developing economy. In general, unit costs of vocational education are found to be higher than those of academic or general education. But because there are different types of vocational training and different institutional arrangements for vocational education (such as vocational schools, company-affiliated vocational schools, schools with a diversified curriculum) in different countries, the difference in cost between the two types of curriculum varies widely. Obviously, cost comparison alone is incomplete for informing the debate over the choice of curriculum in secondary education; the benefits and effects of different curricula have to be taken into account, too.

Cost disparities by curriculum also exist in higher education. Data for a sample of developing countries show that university subjects like agriculture, sciences, and engineering are on the average more than twice as costly as general subjects. And in terms of the magnitude of recurrent cost per pupil, the descending order for the subjects was as follows: agriculture, sciences, engineering, arts, humanities and social sciences. Subjects near the top of the list have higher recurrent expenditures because of lower student-teacher ratios and higher capital expenditures.

For education systems in developing countries, expenditure per pupil exhibits the following patterns: (a) it rises with the level of education; (b) it is dominated by personnel costs, although the proportion for personnel costs decreases with the level of education; (c) it is higher for boarding schools than for day schools at the secondary level; (d) it is generally higher for vocational education than for academic education at the secondary level; (e) it is higher for engineering and science subjects than for arts and humanities at the tertiary level; and (f) it has a built-in tendency to rise over time.

*Source:* Adapted from Tsang, 1988, pp. 204–205

While unit cost analysis is important in putting together the budget proposals for education, costs alone cannot dictate the eventual decisions. As Box 14 below shows, the training priorities for investment in education have to be assessed on many different criteria.

reinforce the other: it is easier for graduates of the formal school system with a solid grounding in theory to specialise in different trades later on. The two may also be alternatives: many skills can be acquired either in a specialised institute or on the job. Where this is the case the relative cost of skill formation in the two loci will be crucial in deciding where training should take place.

**Supplementary signals from private demand.** The social cost-benefit signals regarding the desirability of expanding particular types of training can be supplemented by private sector indicators as to where investment in training should take place. When there are long lists of applicants for certain courses and those admitted are only a small fraction of those who are prepared to enroll and pay the fees, there is the presumption that the supply should be expanded.

**Considerations of educational quality.** Once educational costs are brought into the analysis, issues of internal efficiency and educational quality become more apparent. For example, could a graduate of training course X be produced at lower cost? What internal managerial, pedagogical and organisational changes might lead to lower unit costs? Would a lower unit cost mean a decline in educational quality? Conversely, one may even consider an increase in unit costs for the sake of improving the quality of the graduates.

*Source:* Adapted from Psacharopoulos, 1984, pp. 575–78

## How can the Ministry of Education engage in effective negotiation?

Negotiations can be defined as a process that involves two or more parties who are seeking to resolve their conflicting or diverging points of view into a single decision that is mutually satisfying to all parties involved. In a negotiating process there are issues to be addressed and conflicts or divergent views to be resolved. Two or more parties are involved. Each party marshals its case, plans arguments and counter-arguments and assess the power position of its counterpart.

The preparation for and actual negotiating process requires an understanding of the context in which the negotiations are taking place and of the issue to be resolved. In addition, in order to negotiate effectively, it is important to know the interests and objectives of all those involved in the negotiations; to have adequate supporting information and documentation;

and for each party to agree on the negotiating strategy to be employed. The persons negotiating should also be competent in communications skills, be flexible and be able to contribute to establishing a cordial environment for productive deliberations.

Education officials are required to negotiate locally with the Ministry of Finance and sometimes directly with the International Financial Institutions (IFIs). Negotiations involving officials from the Ministries of Education and Finance are, in general, relatively circumscribed. In many cases no negotiations take place at the final allocation of resources to the various sector ministries. Even without this limited negotiating room, education officials can influence decisions on allocations by entering into dialogue with their counterpart finance officials in order to understand different perspectives and to agree on procedures and requirements for a budget that costs elements for the education sector as seen within the wider national development programme.

Some guidelines that education officials can follow for conducting negotiations are listed below:

- It is important to be able to communicate effectively the value of education and human development in the broader socio-economic development of the country and in relation to policy planning;

- Relevant statistical data and supporting documents contribute to strengthening a position taken in the negotiating process;

- It is necessary to stress by providing examples, if necessary, of the efficiency and effectiveness of the Ministry's performance in implementing projects and programmes;

- The presentation should specify priorities and each should be costed in detail;

- The proposed expenditure should be realistic and in keeping with the managerial and technical capacities of the ministry or institution to implement planned activities effectively;

- Extra-budgetary resources already secured or being negotiated should be stated. In negotiating with IFIs, the Ministry or Education sometimes perceives itself to be the less strong partner. This is so for several reasons:

  - IFIs are holding the purse strings;

  - IFIs are usually well-prepared with a large database at their disposal;

– the negotiations are invariably taking place within a larger context of economic policymaking and a range of conditionalities.

However, it is important for Ministries of Education to note that IFIs are very aware of the harsh effects that adjustment policies and measures have had on the social sector. Also, there is a widespread global consciousness of the pivotal role of the social sector in human development. These considerations should give education officials room to negotiate from a position of strength with the IFIs.

Education officials also need to understand the culture and operating procedures of the particular institutions. They should be familiar with all the elements of the project or programmes for which resources are required. They should base their arguments on well prepared project documents that are supported by reliable research findings, objective analyses, and qualitative and quantitative data.

*Source:* Adapted from Commonwealth Secretariat, 1997

---

**Activity 13**

- *Work in two groups: education personnel presenting budget proposals to finance officials. Each group will marshal relevant arguments based on the proposals. In the negotiating process each group should demonstrate a sensitive awareness of the priorities of the other group.*

---

## Summary

The budgetary process is best understood when it is seen both as part of an ongoing national developmental planning exercise and as an annual fiscal measure. The final product, the budget document, assumes less importance in this conceptualisation. If the process is perceived to be the more important aspect, then there is considerable potential for the Ministry of Education to make a more informed bid for national resources. No longer will it acquiesce in arguments such as: 'there is only one national pie and you have to be content with your slice'. It could be in a position to show how national resources could be more equitably distributed, possibly with an expanded conception of education and its role in national development, and even make a case for a different structure of allocations in education.

More emphasis, then, should be placed by the Ministry of Education at all levels on how it formulates and costs its plans. If its targets can be aligned with national goals and its costings are rigourous and accurate, then it will be in a stronger position to bargain for scarce resources. It will also need to prepare thoroughly to ensure it has the skills and quick thinking necessary at negotiating sessions.

These emphases will in turn depend on a spirit of decision-making that takes into account the contribution of persons at all levels of the education system. It is a glaring paradox that schools represent the major project in education, yet principals, teachers and parents are excluded from the budget planning process. Planning is the essential preserve of those who believe they know what is going on in schools. To make more informed budget proposals, Ministry of Education officials need to show that they have incorporated the prioritised needs of all the stakeholders in education.

The spirit of communication and participation that has been shown to be necessary for the budget planning exercise is also in principle necessary for an effectively run Ministry of Education. The conceptualisation of the budget process in a more comprehensive mode than hitherto augurs well for the Ministry of Education to become more knowledgeable about the needs and strengths of its own sector.

## Wrap-up: discussion and extended reflection

### Financial management: a constituent of the management process

- One of the many misconceptions in the management of finance is that it is merely about money, income and expenditure, or budgeting and costing. It is, however, one of the important phases of the management process that helps to relate needs to resources and the implementation process and assists in the achievement of the desired goals. The emphasis here is on *education-driven* rather than on *resource-driven* educational plans, programmes and projects. Most educational innovations in this part of the world are, however, resource-driven.

### Financial management: a staff development strategy

- As already indicated, the process of financial management facilitates organisational planning, co-ordination, control and evaluation. The process thus enables ongoing staff development and this encourages participation of all those involved in organisational activities such as vision-building, evolutionary planning, context-based staff development, initiative-taking, monitoring, supervision, restructuring and reculturing. In other words, everyone in the organisation participates in financial decisions and takes the responsibility of implementing them successfully.

- The effectiveness of any initiative in so far as devolution of financial management is concerned, will not be realised unless it enables involvement of all concerned in the decision-making process. Such an initiative even at territory level does not enable human resource development at various department levels. The management of finance here has moved from one central authority to a similar position at a lower level in the administrative hierarchy. Devolution initiatives should ensure that everyone in the system learns to use funds sensibly and in a more cost-effective manner.

### Budgeting

- In order to manage finance effectively, it is important to have some understanding of the budgeting and costing processes. Budgets are the means through which expenditure is related to needs. It also, therefore, facilitates organisational planning, co-ordination, control and evaluation. Budget, the formal set of figures written on a piece of paper, is the consequence of these activities and becomes a guide to the management of future activities.

- The budgeting process has four phases: budgetary review, forecasting, implementation and evaluation. While it is appropriate to annualise the budget, the process itself is ongoing.

- The main problems in budgeting include turbulent economic climates, often insufficient research-based data, micro- and macro-politics, escalating costs, inflation and devaluation costs, and overambitious projects.

### Costing

- As seen above, budgeting is concerned with drawing up an overall financial plan as a part of the institutional management process. Costing is concerned with determining the specific costs of an educational activity. The focus here is on providing data about the viability of competing activities.

- An educational administrator has to be realistic in developing and implementing a plan, programme or project. He/she has to take into account what resources are available to implement the plan, programme or project in a given period of time. The costing of education is not as easy as costing an annual budget. The annual budget does not give all the information on costs of education.

- Educational costs can be affected by: changes in price level of goods and services, inflation, demographic changes, raising of school leaving age, teachers' salaries, rise in education standards, new policy decisions and demand for higher education.

The management of educational finance is a 'hidden curriculum' and not many people at the school or system levels are involved in it. This discussion emphasises that financial management is a component of the total educational management process. In an interactive fashion it contributes to the achievement of desired goals. It operates best when it takes a partnership and collaborative route and when it is transparent to the stakeholders. If this happens the process of financial management becomes a learning platform.

*Source:* Adapted from Sharma, 1997)

## Suggested reading

Barsotti, F (1992). 'New strategies for formulating the budget' in Ryan S and Brown D (eds.), *Issues and Problems in Caribbean Public Administration*. UWI, St. Augustine: ISER.

Chinapah, V, Löfstedt, J and Weiler, H (1989). 'Integrated Development of Human Resources and Educational Planning' *Prospects*, XIX (4), pp. 467–78.

Commonwealth Secretariat (1997). 'Background and launch of training programme'. Unpublished paper summarising the seminars: Issues in the Financing of Education in the Caribbean Community. London.

Hallak, J (1969). *The analysis of educational costs and expenditure*. UNESCO: IIEP.

National Advisory Council on State and Local Budgeting (1997). *A Framework for Improved State and Local Government Budgeting and Recommended Budget Practices*. http://207.226.185.119/nacslb/framewrk.htm.

Open University (1972). National Income and Economic Policy IV: Social Sciences – A Second Level Course (Units 13–16). Bletchley, Bucks: Open University Press.

Poignant, R (1967). *The Relation of Educational Plans to Economic and Social Planning*. UNESCO: IIEP.

Psacharopoulos, G (1984). *Assessing Training Priorities in Developing Countries – Current Practices and Possible Alternatives*. NY, USA: World Bank.

Republic of Trinidad & Tobago (1995). Draft Estimates of Expenditure for the Year 1996, prepared by the Ministry of Finance. Port of Spain: Government Printery.

Republic of Trinidad & Tobago (1997). Circular No.3, dated May 13th, 1997 – Draft Estimates of Revenue and Expenditure Including the Income and Expenditure of Statutory Boards and Similar Bodies and of the Tobago House of Assembly. Ministry of Finance. Port of Spain: Government Printery.

Sharma, A (1997). 'The Effective Management of Educational Finance'. Paper presented at the Commonwealth Secretariat and USP's IOE Workshop on Financing of Education, 17–21 November, 1997.

Thompson, D, Wood, C, and Honeyman, D (1994). *Fiscal Leadership for Schools*. NY, USA: Longmans.

Tsang, M C (1988). 'Cost Analysis for Educational Policymaking: a Review of Cost Studies in Education in Developing Countries'. *Review of Educational Research*, 43 (1), pp. 5–23.

Weiler, H (1984). 'The Political Economy of Education and Development', *Prospects*, XIV (4), pp. 467–78.

# MODULE 5

# School financing

## Background

During the last 15 to 20 years there has been increased emphasis on patterns of school finance. School finance, however, is a function of school governance. How the educational system is organised and controlled determines the way money is allocated to schools and the way decisions about the release, use and accounting for such funds take place. Ideas about governance have been changing and, consequently, so have ideas about financing. In the Caribbean, in the past, centralised bureaucracies released appointed sums at appointed times for specific purposes in the state sector. Very little decision-making took place at school level where money was concerned, except in the denominational system. Generally, one can say that there has been a global shift towards decentralised conceptions of governance and so we have to consider alternative arrangements for financing schools.

This module consists of 11 sections.

At the end of Section 2, the participant should be able to explain the main factors influencing school governance in the world today.

At the end of Section 6, the reader should be able to explain some key factors in the educational context shaping school governance and financing:

(a) the impact of effectiveness research;

(b) school improvement planning;

(c) decentralisation initiatives.

At the end of Section 10, the participant should be able to:

1. Discuss the pros and cons of different arrangements for financing;

2. Explain the case for decentralisation;

3. Discuss some of the institutional implications of decentralisation for financing;

4. Compare centralised and decentralised arrangements.

At the end of Section 11, the participant should be able to:

1. Explain the voucher system;

2. Assess the possible social and educational impact of a voucher system.

# SECTION 1

## School financing – the general problem today

School financing has become an area of central concern today in both developing and developed countries. Governments, and in some places, districts, communities and taxpayers are concerned with the achievement of value for money in education. This has led to experiments with all sorts of novel ideas for governance and financing of schools.

### Instruction 1

Read the excerpt in Box 1.

---

**Box 1**

In fact, an article in the *Toronto Star* quotes a Conference Board of Canada study which estimates a $4-billion lifetime loss in earning power for the 137,000 students who failed to graduate with the class of 1979 (Crawford, 1993). The same news publication also mentions a January 1993 report of the Liberal Party's Senate and House of Commons Committee on Youth which points out that school drop-outs are a great cost to Canadian taxpayers in terms of their weak earning power, the lower taxes these individuals pay, and the additional costs of unemployment insurance, welfare, health and policing. The Province of Ontario has a $14-billion public school system, comprising $10 billion in provincial spending and another $4 billion collected in local property taxes for the running of schools. The nation, as a whole, has a $55-billion education system. Given such figures, many Canadians are understandably concerned that they are not getting their money's worth in their educational spending.

'Reconstructing "Dropout"'. George J. Sefa Dei, Josephine Mazzuca, Elizabeth Mc Isaac, Jasmine Zine, 1997, p. 8

---

**Activity 1**

1. *Are the above concerns applicable to the USA and UK today?*

2. *What are the concerns about 'value for money' in your own country?*

3. *How do these concerns express themselves in your country?*

# SECTION 2

## The present world context

How much money individual schools get for financing their needs and how that money is accessed, allocated and accounted for depends partly on the current set of ideas which dominate thinking in the field.

*Instruction 2*

Read Box 2.

---

**Box 2**

Some dominant ideas influencing school management and governance and by extension school financing include:

1. Confidence in central planning has decreased with the collapse of the communist regions of Eastern Europe and the poor record of state run institutions in other parts of the world.

2. Growth of new technology has made it more possible than ever before to take decisions at relatively local levels. With information technology it has become easier to reconcile genuine local autonomy with strategic control at the central level.

3. The rise of the neo-liberal paradigm which emphasises competition and 'survival of the fittest' encourages decentralisation of school management.

4. The recent experience of recession and structural adjustment in many developing economies has reduced the amount of money available for educational expenditures and has produced great emphasis on accountability and efficiency.

---

**Activity 2**

1. *Do you see evidence already that the factors cited in Box 2 are influencing school financing?*

2. *Check any recent development plan for education in your country. What changes are being proposed for school governance and financing?*

---

# SECTION 3

## The educational context

During the 1960s, sociological studies produced in the USA suggested that the influence of the home was the key factor in determining educational success. This led to many policies aimed at compensating for socio-economic deficiencies. The last 15 years have seen a rethinking on the potency of the individual school unit as an agent for producing educational change. This rethinking was due to effective schools research and the application of strategic planning techniques to educational administration.

### Instruction 3

Read Box 3.

---

**Box 3**

The last 15 years have seen a rethinking of the thesis originally propounded by American social scientists Coleman *et al.* (1966) and Jencks et al. (1972) that the effect that schools could have on the academic achievement (and therefore life chances) of the children in them was strictly limited compared with the effects of family background, and that schools in capitalist economies by and large simply reproduced the social class structure of that society. But research carried out in the United States and in the United Kingdom has shown that effective schools do enable their pupils to make more progress than might have been expected given their social background, and that others do the reverse. New statistical techniques have enabled researchers to calculate what level of achievement a pupil is likely to reach, given history of her previous attainment and socio-economic status – and what the expected performance of a school might be, given what kind of pupils it has. Then the actual level of performance can be compared with the expected level. This concept of an identifiable 'school effect' has been taken on board by a number of evaluation agencies in different countries, including the French Ministry of Education's Direction de l'Evaluation et de la Prospective (DEP).

OECD, *Schools Under Scrutiny,* 1996, p. 20

---

**Activity 3**

1. How did 'effectiveness research' change the outlook on schools?
2. How could the findings of this research lead to more school autonomy?
3. What consequences could 1 and 2 above have for school financing?

---

# SECTION 4

## The educational content

### *Instruction 4*

Read Box 4.

---

**Box 4**

In such a climate of change and strenuous self-improvement, the school itself is emerging as an important axis in the effort to evaluate and improve the performance of the education system. First, it is a convenient unit for financial accountability – especially since some education systems have been restructured, first to shift financial responsibilities from central to local government and secondly, in some cases, to push budgetary management even further from the centre, out to the schools themselves. It is also an appropriate unit through which to establish accountability to parents and the community – both in conceptual and operational terms. The public in most countries is familiar with the concept of 'good' and 'bad' schools – institutions which are or are not fulfilling the function society is paying them to carry out – and often make such judgements themselves. At the same time, schools are educative communities, in which shifts in ethos, climate or approach can have a substantial effect on the quality of learning in the institution.

Direct pressure can be put on individual schools to change their mode of operation, or improve their performance, which is hard to do with intermediate layers such as local education boards, municipalities or school districts. School principals and teachers, governors and trustees, are often highly visible in the local community and personally as well as structurally accountable in a way that local government officers, and even elected representatives, are not. This makes the school as a unit a powerful location for improving the quality of a system.

*Schools Under Scrutiny, op. cit.*

---

**Activity 4**

1. *What factors make the individual school an important axis for policy implementation and evaluation?*

2. *How would this affect the drive to autonomy for schools?*

3. *What will be the implications for financing?*

# SECTION 5

## The educational content

*Instruction 5*

Read Box 5.

---

**Box 5**

In the accelerated school the stress is on the school as a whole rather than on a particular grade, curriculum, approach to teacher training, or other more limited strategy. The organisational approach assumes that the strategy must do three things: (1) develop a unity of purpose among all of the participants; (2) 'empower' all of the major participants and raise their feelings of efficacy and responsibility for the outcomes of the school; and (3) build on the considerable strengths of the participants rather than decrying their weaknesses.

Unity of purpose refers to agreement among parents, teachers, and students with respect to a common set of goals for the school that will be the focal point of everyone's efforts.

Empowerment refers to the ability of the key participants to make important decisions at the school level and in the home to improve the education of students. It is based upon breaking the present stalemate among administrators, teachers, parents and students in which the participants tend to blame each other, as well as factors 'beyond their control', or the poor educational outcomes of disadvantaged students.

An accelerated school must build upon an expanded role for all groups to participate and take responsibility for the educational process and results. Such an approach requires a shift to school-based decision making with heavy involvement of teachers and parents and new administrative roles. Building of strengths refers to employing all the learning resources that students, parents, school staff, and communities can bring to the educational endeavour.

Henry Leven, *Effective Schools*, Chapter 9

---

**Activity 5**

1. *Summarise the main tenets of school improvement planning listed here.*
2. *What approach to school management is articulated?*
3. *What are the consequences for governance of schools as well as financing of schools?*

# SECTION 6

## The educational content

### Instruction 6

Read Boxes 6 and 7.

Another recent feature which has placed emphasis on the school as an individual unit has been the rise of decentralisation as a technique for school improvement.

---

**Box 6**

- a shift from the use of input controls and bureaucratic procedures and rules to a reliance on quantifiable output measures and performance targets;
- the devolution of management control coupled with the development of new reporting, monitoring and accountability mechanisms;
- the disaggregation of large bureaucratic structures into quasi-autonomous agencies;
- the imitation of certain private sector management practices such as corporate plans, performance agreements and mission statements, the development of new management information systems;
- a stress on cost cutting and efficiency.

*Schools Under Scrutiny, op. cit.,* p. 19

---

**Box 7**

Decentralisation can take the form of de-concentration, delegation and devolution (Rondenelli, 1981) – all involving the transfer of central government authority and its tasks and function to other bodies (Winkler, 1986). De-concentration involves a transfer of lower levels within the central government – such as the creation of regional directorates in the ministry of education. Delegation involves a transfer to organisations outside the central government – such as training agencies and universities. In both cases, the federal government continues to be the main source of financing. Devolution involves a transfer to autonomous and independent sub-national units of government – such as provinces, cities and districts – which are empowered both to raise tax revenues and to spend them. The outcome is often a school system financed and controlled by the local government.

Emanuel Jiminez and Jee Peng Tan, 'Decentralised and Private Education: The Case of Pakistan', *Comparative Education,* Vol. 23, No. 2, 1987, p. 174

---

**Activity 6**

1. How would the application of ideas in Box 6 make individual schools more responsible for their own performances?

2. Study the different possible levels of decentralisation in Box 7 and clarify the implication for governance and financing in each case.

# SECTION 7

## Options for school financing

'Alternative models of government intervention in education can generally be characterised according to the way schools are managed and financed. The sharpest distinction is between public and private schools. In a privatised system of education, schools derive their revenue entirely from fees and other private contributions, and are free to determine the type of educational services offered. In contrast, schools in a purely public system show the opposite features: they are managed directly by government and their expenditure are met by tax revenues'.

Emmanuel Jiminez and Jee Peng Tan, op. cit., p. 174

Study Box 8.

## Box 8

### Table 5.1. A Typology of the Organisation of School Systems

| Feature | Private sector | | Public sector | | |
|---|---|---|---|---|---|
| | **Public private model** | **Mixed model** | **Pure decentralised model** | **Mixed model** | **Pure centralised model** |
| *Finance* | | | | | |
| a) Revenue source | Private contributions (tuitions and other fees) | Private contributions plus government grants and resources-in-kind | Local government own-source revenues | Local government own-source revenues plus grants from higher levels of government and resources-in-kind | Full central government funding |
| b) Method of financing | All school inputs financed by school revenues | Some school inputs (for example teachers) financed by grants and in-kind contributed from government | School inputs financed by local government revenues | Some school inputs provided in kind by higher levels | All school inputs provided directly in kind to schools |
| *Management* | | | | | |
| a) Decisions on level and type of spending | Decisions set by school and reflecting preferences of school clientele | Decisions of school subject to control by government | Local government autonomy to decide according to preferences of local residents | Local government decisions constrained by higher government regulations | Decisions set by central government |
| (b) Fee policy | Fees set at level reflecting market forces | Fee ceiling imposed by government | Local government autonomy in setting fees | Fees charged are subject to control by higher levels of government | No fees are levied |
| (c) Service provision | Free choice constraint in curricula | Some constraint on curricula | Local choice in curricula | Local choice limited by regulations of higher levels of government | Standard national curriculum for all schools |

## Activity 7

1. Given all that you have read in this module so far which is the point in this typology that countries seem to be gravitating toward?

2. What are the advantages of a purely centralised model?

3. Can you come up with a framework for deciding which model of school finance is suitable to your country?

4. Are there schools in your country operating according to the pure private model?

5. How did the present arrangements for financing schools evolve historically in your country?

6. Would decentralisation ease the burden on state financing?

7. Can decentralisation be structured to maximise the use of private and community funding?

# SECTION 8

*Instruction 8*

Read Box 9.

Advantages of decentralisation

---

**Box 9**

(a) Local control evidently encourages responsiveness to local needs.

(b) Even at the level of the individual school or college, differences of geography, resources, tradition and personal preference imply a need for some kinds of significant decision to be within the powers of local management.

(c) Decentralisation can speed up the decision making process. If minor issues have to be referred to some remote central authority, rapid response is out of the question.

(d) Decentralisation, therefore, encourages the development of a clear distinction between strategic control which is the proper function of the centre and operational management which is more effectively carried out locally. This distinction in turn helps to create an organisational structure which is both effective and responsive. It should be noticed, however, that the separation of strategy and operational control may in practice be difficult to achieve.

(e) A serious problem in highly centralised systems is one of scale. The sheer number of individual schools or the size of the area mean that the issues are frequently beyond the comprehension of even perfectly capable administrators.

(f) Decentralisation encourages initiative and improves the quality of management, particularly at local level. In a highly centralised system key figures such as district officers or headteachers are denied decision making opportunities and frequently have little, if any, management training. Their quality of management is, therefore, not surprisingly, often poor.

---

(g) Decentralisation releases human potential. People respond to increased opportunities to use their talents and energies productively.

(h) Greater involvement in the decision making process improves morale leading to enhanced job satisfaction and better motivation.(i) A well designed system of decentralised management increases accountability. Clarifying the respective roles of central government, local government, school management and other agencies makes it possible to set appropriate targets for each.

Kier Bloomer, *Decentralising the Education System.* Commonwealth Secretariat, 1991, p. 3

## Activity 8

1. *Do these advantages of decentralisation hold in your education system?*

2. *What aspect of your education system should still be centralised?*

# SECTION 9

## Local financial management

### Instruction 9

In the event that decentralising does take place, there must be some restructuring of financial control to accord more autonomy to the individual school.

Read Box 10.

---

**Box 10**

9.6.1 Ultimately any system of delegation is likely to involve some decentralisation of decision concerning money. Indeed, any restructuring which stops short of developing some measure of financial control will be restricted to administrative decentralisation. The element of empowering local people will be minimised.

9.6.2 If the government is contemplating some measure of local financial management a very wide range of issues will need to be addressed, including the following:

(i) To which level or levels is control to be devolved? Will individual districts and/or schools have their own budgets?

(ii) What areas of budgetary control are to be devolved? For example, districts could be given control over repairs and maintenance but not over new buildings. Schools might control the supply of teaching materials but not classroom equipment over a certain value.

(iii) How are minimum standards to be prescribed and what levels of discretion will be permitted? For example, in relation to teacher staff it might be laid down that for a school of a certain size finance will be provided to allow the employment of ten teachers. The school or district might have discretion to vary the actual complement in response to local needs and priorities but subject to a prescribed minimum and maximum.

(iv) On what basis are local budgets to be assessed? What account is to be taken of factors such as numbers of pupils, numbers of schools, travel difficulties etc?

(v) What arrangements can be made for auditing?

*Decentralising the Education System, op. cit.,* p. 10

---

## SECTION 10

### Key values affecting policy on school financing

In assessing the options of centralised types of control and financing and decentralised types of control and financing the same aims are advanced to support either options. Protagonists of both camps argue for the same objectives.

*Instruction 10*

Read Box 11.

# SECTION 11

## Radical options for school financing

### *Quasi-markets*

The theory of quasi-markets is premised on the assumptions that the introduction of market-oriented policies in education will foster competition, encourage a more economical use of resources, make producers more accountable to consumers, increase choice and promote diversity and provide a better deal for the poor. The philosophy beneath it all is the doctrine of competition and 'survival of the fittest', i.e. make schools compete, give parents power as consumers, make teachers accountable and let the system become self-driven.

### *Instruction 11*

Read Boxes 12 and 13.

**Box 12**

A tax-funding education voucher in the broadest sense is a payment made by the government to a school chosen by the parent of the child being educated; the voucher finances all or most of the tuition charged. The system introduces competition among public schools and between public and private schools; and it enables schools to offer diverse educational packages to meet the different preferences of parents.

E. West, 'Education Voucher in Principle and Practice: A Survey'. *World Bank Research Observer*, Vol. 12, No. 1, p. 83

## Box 13

### The Rationale for Voucher Systems

The goal of all voucher plans – to provide families with maximum choice within a decentralised and competitive system of schools – embodies four principles: consumer choice, personal advancement, the promotion of competition, and equal opportunity. Consumer choice, in education, equals parental choice: parents choose schools for their children by virtue of their parental authority and are thus, in a fundamental sense, the real consumers of education. Under a voucher plan, government serves the consumers of education – parents – rather than the suppliers of education – school.

The second principle, that of personal advancement, is rooted in the conviction that people want to shape their own destinies. The opportunity to choose and to decide stimulates interest, participation, enthusiasm and dedication. Many government programmes – for example social security, welfare, health programmes, student loans – directly subsidise the individual recipients with funding for services among which they can select. Social security recipients, for example, can spend their cheques however they choose. The goal of educational vouchers is to extend this principle to education.

The third principle, the stimulation of competition, applies here because public schools are usually monopolies. The objective of vouchers is to challenge them to compete – with each other and with private school – through reducing costs, increasing quality, and introducing dynamic innovation.

The fourth principle – the goal of equality of opportunity – underlying the rationale for vouchers is a logical outcome of the other three and is expressed in the objective of increasing access to private schools. This goal is embodied particularly in those selective, or targeted voucher schemes that give low-income families greater access to private schools.

E. West, *op. cit.*, p. 85

## Activity 11

1. *Summarise the arguments for a voucher system.*
2. *Would the argument advanced for a voucher system hold in your country?*
3. *How would a voucher system affect the poor in the long run?*

## Suggested reading

Bloomer, Keer (1991). *Decentralising the Education System*. Commonwealth Secretariat.

Carnoy, Martin (1997). 'Is privatisation through education vouchers really the answer? A comment', *World Bank Research Observer*, Vol. 12, No. 1, pp. 108–16.

Cambron-McLabe, Melda H and Odden, Allan (eds.) (1982). *The Changing Politics of School Finance*. American Finance Association.

Jiminez, Emmanuel and Jee Pen Tan. 'Decentralised and Private Education: The Case of Pakistan', *Comparative Education*, Vol. 23, No. 2, pp. 173–90.

Odden, Allan (ed.) (1992). *Rethinking School Finance*. San Francisco: Jossey-Bass Publishers.

OECD (1996). *Schools Under Scrutiny*.

Rogen, Martin (1992). *Opting Out: Choice and the Future of Schools*. London: Laurence and Wishart.

West, E G (1997). 'Education Vouchers in Principle and Practice: A Survey', *World Bank Research Observer*, Vol. 12, No. 1, pp. 83–98.

# MODULE 6

## Accountability

### Overview

Most people, lay and professional alike, agree that the education sector should receive a large percentage of a country's investment. Since the advent of human capital theories this has indeed been the case in many countries of the developing world. However, emphasis on such heavy capital outlay must at some point be shown to be justified, and there must be evidence that money has been well invested, because for most of these countries resources are scarce. Yet many countries have so far been unable to undertake a thorough evaluation of their education systems. Such an evaluation would seek to determine whether the system had been *efficient* in its use of the country's resources, whether it had made *equity* gains for different sectors of the population and whether it had been used to improve the *quality* of education in the country. These are the accountability issues on which an education system needs to be evaluated.

The obvious task in evaluating an education system would be to assess its outcome – i.e. student achievement. How is this to be done? Clearly, testing is the answer. Thus, this chapter will discuss some issues relevant to the design and construction of tests. Tests, however, serve different functions. For example, they may be used for selection purposes or for the gaining of credentials, or they may be designed to give an indication of the health of the system. Some idea of the basic differences in tests will be developed. Once a test has been implemented and scored through, how are the results to be interpreted? This takes us into the highly contentious world of 'standards'. Here we find that many people have only a hazy idea of what standards are and yet continually make judgements based on them. This module will show that standards have to be carefully selected, assessed and monitored if they are to be used in evaluating the system.

If we succeed in all these efforts, the unhappy fact remains that we still do not have a complete assessment of the education system. We need to engage in cross-national comparisons to see how our efforts measure up with those of others striving for similar goals – otherwise, it would be only a self-contained endeavour. This chapter will look at the kind of information generated by surveys conducted by the IEA (International Evaluation of Educational Assessment) as a measure of how the system is functioning.

## Objectives

When s/he has completed this module, the participant should be able to:

1. Justify, in the context of educational financing, the need to set up evaluations of education systems.

2. Explain how national attainment tests differ from those designed for other purposes.

3. Interpret indicators of system performance.

4. Critically appraise the notion of 'standards' in the assessment of educational achievement.

5. Justify the need to include comparative international educational indices of assessment for purposes of accountability.

6. Demonstrate an awareness of the procedures and mechanisms which guarantee accountability, not just for compliance, but in the interests of efficiency, equity and improvement in the education system.

## Accountability and educational financing

The education system can be assessed on its efforts to realise efficiency, equity and quality or improvements, in the delivery of education to the country. These are the reasons for which it was financed. These are the tasks an education system is required to perform and for which it is accountable .

**Efficiency** has to do with whether the system is maintaining or increasing its output of graduates at every level in a cost-effective manner. It would thus examine student-teacher and enrolment ratios, different ways of transmitting curricula, different curricula, drop-out and repetition rates, and graduation rates. Such indicators need to be periodically monitored to give policy makers a real sense of whether the system is doing what it is supposed to do cost-effectively. They may well suggest that more funding may be necessary in some areas for the system to become more efficient in producing output.

**Equity** is concerned with whether all groups in the society are being treated fairly by the education system. Hence, no group should be over-represented as graduates at any level of the system or appear to be confined to certain types of schools. This hinges on the clear correlation between educational credentials and well-paying jobs, leading to a higher standard of living. Equity, then, is really a means of measuring to what extent all groups are able to access social mobility. Governments expect that the heavy financial investment they have made in education is one indirect, long-term way of addressing this issue and the system must therefore deliver.

**Quality** indicators have to do with pedagogy and the nature of the education that is being transmitted. Are the curricular programmes designed for, and relevant to, the age and interests of the students? Is the teaching innovative and stimulating? Are most teachers trained? Is the learning and knowledge helpful in developing critical thinkers and productive citizens? The improvement of instructional practices also has implications for improving the efficiency of the system, so that efficiency and quality indicators are closely related.

All countries seem to invest heavily in education. National goals may vary from country to country, but all countries want their education systems to be efficient, equitable and capable of delivering a 'quality' education. Hence, the system has to be evaluated to see how well it is performing on these indicators. Especially in small developing countries, planners and policy makers in need to become aware of, and insist on the need for, the establishment of procedures and mechanisms to guarantee accountability in the education system.

## Accountability and achievement indicators

The issue of accountability in education is bound up with the dominance of academic achievement as its major output indicator. The notion of achievement is not at issue because this is, after all, the major project of schools – to educate students and then test them on what they have learned. However, there is some dissatisfaction with the specific indicator most in use today, that of cognitive or intellectual achievement. Box 1 below discusses some of the issues surrounding output indicators.

**Box 1**

**Choice of Outcome Indicators**

To enumerate the outcomes of education about which it might be useful to have empirical information in terms of the many aims that have been posited for education would be an endless task. Aims frequently suggested include the development of literacy and numeracy skills, the development of aesthetic areas of experience, preparation for life in a democratic society, preparation for the world of work, development of character and moral sensitivity and personal self-fulfilment. Aims (and expected outcomes) may differ for different ages and students. Given the range of educational aims and the complexity and difficulty of measuring outcomes, some selection has to be made in deciding what outcomes should be measured for use in an indicator system. All we can hope for is information on a limited number of indicators rather than a description of all possible outcomes.

In choosing indicators, the evaluator will be influenced by consideration of which educational outcomes are regarded as important and by the ease and efficiency with which the outcomes can be measured. Thus, both political and technical considerations have to be attended to. At the political level, some measures will be regarded as more important or credible than others, and achieving consensus on these may not be easy. At the technical level, considerations relating to such factors as method of measurement, sampling strategies, and how data are aggregated and reported may also constrain the selection of indicators. . . .

The role of both political and technical factors is evident in the emphasis placed on cognitive factors in assessing school outcomes. Partly because it is difficult to obtain agreement on the value as school outcomes of activities with a large noncognitive component, and partly because these activities are difficult to measure, most attention in the development of outcome measures has been given to cognitive achievement. The general public, as well as those professionally involved in education, seems genuinely interested in finding out what cognitive skills and knowledge students have acquired in school. For example, can students read and write satisfactorily? Is their knowledge of science and technology adequate for life in the contemporary world?

*Source:* Adapted from Greaney and Kellaghan, 1996, pp. 4–5

Cognitive testing, however, is not without its array of problematic issues. Since the evaluation of achievement on a national scale is likely to be an expensive undertaking, decisions have to be made about selecting some areas of competence to test. Which subject areas are more inclined to give key insights into the performance of the system against the goals of efficiency, equity and quality? The key subject areas that are normally chosen are English, mathematics, science and social studies. They represent areas of the curriculum that are considered core subjects and therefore most students have been exposed to them. National testing in subjects offered only by some students, for example art or technical-vocational studies, is of limited value.

Important decisions also have to be made about the frequency with which this exercise should be undertaken. Is it feasible to run the same tests every year to get an idea of trends over time, or is it just as feasible to do so in cycles four or five years apart? What kind of designs should be used in the assessment of student achievement? Cross-sectional designs will garner information on how students are performing in certain subjects across the nation at one point in time. Longitudinal designs, on the other hand, provide data for the same (or different) cohorts at certain intervals over time? Which should be chosen if both analysis of outputs and monitoring of learning is required?

## Summary

This introduction to testing in the context of establishing accountability of the educational system, shows it to be an extremely specialized subject. Competent personnel in the field of testing and measurement are needed to design procedures and mechanisms that facilitate meaningful evaluation of national education systems. The sections below will address some of the specialist knowledge needed in the field of test construction and information needed in the analysis of results. The latter, however, is not an 'exact science' as it rests on values inherent in the selection, monitoring and evaluation of standards. Hence, accountability in educational systems not only rests with statisticians and measurement personnel but also with those knowledgeable about the workings of the whole system – the planners and policy makers in education and finance.

## Testing

**Distinguishing between different kinds of tests** – Box 2 below summarises the variety of tests that exists in a school system and the purposes for which they have been constructed. Tests designed for evaluation of national educational systems must differ in fundamental ways from tests taken by primary school students to select those to go on to secondary education, or tests taken to obtain credentials at the end of secondary school.

## Box 2

### Testing and Evaluations of Educational Systems

Tests are the most common measure of student learning and are typically used to monitor learning. Tests are defined as 'any series of questions or exercises or other means of measuring the skill, knowledge, intelligence, capacities or aptitudes of an individual or group' (Anderson, Ball and Murphy, 1975, p. 425). Education achievement tests focus on skills, knowledge and capacities that students acquire through education (schooling). They do not seek to measure intelligence or aptitude.

Psychometricians construct educational achievement tests for many different purposes, of which the most common are:

- Monitoring achievement trends over time;
- Evaluating specific educational programs or policies;
- Holding schools, regions, and other administrative sub-units accountable for student achievement;
- Selecting students for further education;
- Certifying student achievement;
- Diagnosing individual learning needs.

The purpose of the test determines its overall design, for example, the purpose of selection tests is to discriminate between individuals, and hence the test will include many items of a difficulty known to discriminate between those who should be selected and those who should not. As a consequence, the range of competencies tested will be highly constrained. By comparison, the purpose of a test designed to monitor national achievement is to assess a large number of competency areas, but to provide little information about specific individuals. It will include items covering many competencies, but its power to discriminate among individuals will be constrained. Tests designed to monitor trends over time will repeat at least some items, whereas tests designed only to select once need not be equated.

*Source:* Adapted from Lockheed, 1996, pp. 10–11

## Activity 1

*Consider the kinds of tests that occur in your country or region. Classify them according to the six criteria listed in Box 2. Is there evidence of any evaluation of the national education system? If there is not, what are the reasons for this? If there is, investigate:*

*1. How recently this practice was established;*

*2. What subject areas have been tested;*

*3. How the actual test items differ from those in other kinds of tests;*

*4. At what levels in the system it has been considered feasible to test.*

## National assessment

National assessment testing also differs from high-stakes selection or credentialling tests in that a great volume of back-up data is collected so that test results can be appropriately interpreted by planners and policy makers, educators, parents and the public in general. Box 3 below elaborates on the data required by national assessments and how they are used.

## Box 3

### National Assessments and Background Data

Educational assessments include not only measures of student learning, but also of student background and school inputs and processes that enable the assessment data to be used for policy analysis. Many researchers have sought to identify the minimum set of information that should be collected. Most recommend the collection of basic intellectual, socio-economic, and cultural background data on students. Examples include the students' sex, age, nutritional status, socio-economic status, language, attitudes, expectations and ability. Theory, research and experience suggest four areas about which data on classroom inputs should be gathered: the curriculum, instructional materials, adequate time for learning and effective teaching . . . Beyond these inputs are (a) managerial processes at the schools and within the classroom, such as tracking, school structure, and autonomy; and (b) school context conditions such as student access to knowledge, organisational press for achievement, and professional teaching conditions.

*Source:* Adapted from Lockheed, 1996, p. 14

## Contextual information

There are several reasons why information other than information on student achievement should be obtained in national assessments. Firstly, the quality of resources, people and activities in school is important in itself. Secondly, only a small range of educational outputs can be measured and the use of contextual information may prevent schools from placing undue emphasis on the outputs measured to the exclusion of other important factors. And thirdly, by allowing an examination of the interactions of inputs, processes and outputs, contextual information may provide clues to policy makers about why schools obtain the outcomes that they do.

Several kinds of contextual information are likely to be of value in providing clues to policy makers about the determinants of achievement, particularly determinants that might be alterable through changes in educational policy. It is interesting to know what students bring to school from their family and community backgrounds that may contribute to successful or poor school performance. One cannot assume, however, that factors found to be important in one cultural context will be of similar importance in other contexts. For example, the fairly consistent conclusions from industrial countries in Europe and North America that family size is negatively related to educational achievement has not been found in studies in Kenya or in Tanzania. In these countries a positive rather than a negative relationship was found between family size and educational achievement, measured in a variety of ways.

*Source:* Adapted from Greaney and Kellaghan, 1996, pp. 35–36

---

### Activity 2

*Investigate the research evidence on the distribution of educational resources (for example physical plant, curricula, libraries, laboratories) in different countries and their record of educational achievement.*

* *Compare the data from developed and developing countries.*

* *Are there indications that a wide array of contextual data is valuable in formatting analyses of achievement patterns?*

## Public examinations

Public examinations differ markedly from national assessments because their purposes vary. National assessments are conducted to monitor the levels of equity, efficiency and quality education in the system and require a host of contextual data. Public examinations discriminate between students who are then sorted and allocated within the system. They are regarded as high-stakes examinations and largely determine the life-chances of students. National assessments are low-stakes. They give only an indication about the functioning of the system, and only a sample of students need be tested. However, the tests are comprehensive in covering the curriculum because assessors need to know how well students are doing on all curricular objectives. Public examinations, on the other hand, involve all students in a year group and differentiate between students of different abilities rather than gauge whether curricular objectives have been met.

## The nature of the instrument

Testing is a precise activity. The test is referred to as an instrument that measures performance or achievement. Boxes 4, 5 and 6 below discuss some of the criteria involved in the construction and administration of tests – i.e. standardisation procedures, reliability and validity considerations and item discrimination. These procedures are necessary to ensure that there is equity in testing – that all students sitting the examination are dealt with in a fair way. Such precautions are absolutely vital when tests are being administered across the country in all kinds of schools and contexts as well as when they are being administered over time to different groups so that comparability can be maintained.

---

**Box 4**

**Testing and Standardisation Procedures**

Tracking progress requires having tools capable of monitoring trends over time. Tests must be standardised with respect to content, behavioural objectives, format, administration procedures, and scoring. Standardising the content requires that the same or equivalent questions or performance tasks be posed for all students. Standardising test administration requires uniformity in the written and verbal instructions given to examinees, in the length of time afforded them, in the materials provided to them, and in the physical testing environment. Standardised scoring requires explicit, impartial procedures for correcting tests or judging performance.

*Source:* Adapted from Lockheed, 1996, p. 12

---

Other than being standardised, test instruments need to be valid and reliable, whether for public examinations or national assessments. The excerpt in Box 5 explains the difference between the two concepts, and the importance of both, in test construction.

**Box 5**

**Testing and Considerations of Reliability and Validity**

An instrument is reliable if it measures whatever it measures accurately and consistently, but it is valid if it measures what it is expected to measure and does so accurately and consistently. Consider the following example. Suppose a country's ministry of education has the following telephone numbers:

| | |
|---|---|
| Minister | 042-770-504, 042-771-345 |
| Permanent Secretary | 042-771-640 |
| Secretary to the Minister | 042-771-500 |

Suppose that when you dial the minister's number each time you reach the minister's secretary. The telephone has not given you what you wanted, but it has been accurate and consistent in what it has given. It is a reliable phone. However, it is not valid because it has not delivered what you wanted, namely, getting through on the minister's line. If, however, each time you dial 042-770-504 the phone on the minister's desk rings, then it is valid because it is giving you what you wanted in accurate and consistent manner. Observe also that, in this case, the phone is also reliable because it is accurate and consistent. In general, if an instrument is valid, it is necessarily reliable. If, by contrast, when you dial 042-770-504 and reach 042-771-345, 042-771-640, 042-771-720, or 042-771-250 at various times, then the phone is neither reliable nor valid.

Reliability is usually established by using such methods as test-retest, equivalent forms, split half, and the Kuder-Richardson formula. As for validities, these may be of different types, for example, concurrent, predictive, face, and content. An important aspect of any national assessment is that the utmost care is taken to ensure the acceptability and accuracy of the outcomes.

*Source:* Adapted from Nwama, 1996, p. 25

---

## Activity 4

- *Investigate at least one statistical method, mentioned in Box 5, of establishing test reliability. Create a test in a curriculum area in which you are familiar. Assess its reliability characteristics.*

- *Examine the differences between the different kinds of test validity mentioned above. Use the test you have created to illustrate at least one kind of validity check.*

- *Attempt to justify to an audience, who is unaware of the procedures involved in test creation, the importance of designing reliable and valid measuring tools.*

---

Whether high or low stakes, tests are instruments which must be precisely put together if they are to be taken seriously as generating informative output indicators. Standardisation procedures, issues of validity and reliability and item analysis then become major features of testing. Box 6 below discusses some of the concerns inherent in item writing.

## Box 6

### Testing and Item Analysis

Care is also taken to ensure that items are free from cultural, racial, religious, gender, and location bias. This is extremely important because research has shown that seemingly neutral achievement test items may actually favour one subcultural group or handicap another. In multi-ethnic and geographically diverse situations, as is the case in developing Africa, this factor does operate and test developers must recognise it and guard against it. This can be done through detailed item critiques and revisions.

*Source:* Adapted from Nwama, 1996, p. 26

### Dangers of Cultural Bias in Testing

The following problem was given to a sample of adolescents and adults as part of a pretest in a study of basic learning needs in Bangladesh:

*Abu owned thirty-two bighas of land. When he died his land was divided evenly among his wife, daughter and two sons. How much land did his daughter get?*

Succession and property rights under the laws of the two main religious groups that apply in Bangladesh would prompt respondents to offer answers other than 8 bighas. Under Islamic law, the mother gets one-eighth of the property and each daughter gets half as much as each son. Under Hindi law, the daughter receives nothing if there are sons in the family.

*Source:* Adapted from Greaney and Kellaghan, 1996, p. 60

## Activity 5

*Item writing is a technical and specialised task.*

- *Research the topic of item writing and suggest other kinds of criteria (other than cultural bias) which are important in creating items for examinations.*

- *Review any test that you can procure from primary or secondary schools or from a public testing agency. Critically assess the test items against the criteria you have researched.*

- *Should informal classroom tests to monitor learning be designed with the same kind of rigour of formal tests? Survey some teachers in the system to get a sense of how they approach testing.*

## Designs of national assessments

Countries may adopt a cross-sectional or longitudinal design, or some type of compromise in its evaluation of the system. Whatever design is adopted depends on what resources the country commands and what kinds of questions it wants answered. Although only a sample is involved in national assessments, considerable investment in the project is still required. Box 7 below explores some of the emphases, strengths and shortcomings of each type of design.

---

**Box 7**

**Survey Design Issues**

Implicit in a decision to do a cross-sectional study is a focus on the cumulative learning of children, either up to the particular grade of school or by a particular age. Implicit in a design to do a repeated-measurement study (or longitudinal design) is a focus on instructional characteristics affecting learning within the time period bounded by the time points of measurement – namely, the beginning and end of the selected grade of school.

**Focus of a cross-sectional study** – Most IEA (International Evaluation of Educational Assessment) studies have had a cross-sectional design, corresponding to fundamental interest in assessing and comparing cumulative achievement in a subject area as attained by students when they reach a given grade or age. The content domain has been defined as the essential core of the subject area as it accumulates and culminates at the target grade or year. We want to know in detail what students know and can do. The explanatory variables are personal (what kinds of students have what levels of attainment) and systemic (what school and teaching circumstances lead to higher achievements). The educational policy inferences are general and structural: for example, they deal with curricular arrangements, tracking and specialisation, retention and yield.

The effects of education are strongly cumulative and all of the learning that have been attained by a particular age or stage of schooling are a consequence of what has gone on before. Only if longitudinal study designs are used is it conceptually possible to isolate effects that occur within a specified, grade-year-limited time period and even this is a methodologically difficult task. As a consequence, explanations of cross-sectional data on achieved learning must rest on events that have occurred during the earlier as well as the contemporaneous process of schooling.

---

Focus of a longitudinal study – The fundamental interest is in the processes and connections of teaching and learning in the content area at the target grade level. The content domain is defined by what is being taught at the grade level. We want to know in detail about cognitive growth, about what students learn during the target year. The explanatory variables are the student input characteristics (prior attitudes and prior knowledge) and grade-specific measures of curriculum and pedagogy (content opportunities, teaching and classroom practices, teacher knowledge and student activities). The educational policy inferences are specific and formative: for example, they deal with the appropriateness of different content domains, with pacing and differentiation of content, with teaching methods and with student work.

Adapted from Wiley and Wolfe, 1992, pp. 297–300

---

## Activity 6

*Consider these tasks:*

- *If you had to design a national assessment in a specific content area for your country, for a particular level of schooling, which survey design would you choose?*

- *Justify your decision in relation to the characteristics of the particular country, especially its needs, resources and the general context of education.*

---

## Standards

### *The range of interpretations of the term 'standards'*

It is often heard nowadays that 'standards are falling'. What are standards? Are they synonymous with national examination results, so that if more students do poorly on a test compared to a decade ago, we can say that the standard has fallen over time? They are also referred to as 'benchmarks of excellence' – could it then be the criteria used by examining bodies to allocate grades? Thus, only raw scores of 80 and over will be deemed worthy of an 'A'? Or, on the other hand, standards may not be related to final events like exams and grading procedures, but may actually refer to the teaching and learning processes in classrooms – are the expectations of teachers and the methods they employ conducive to learning for the majority of students?

In most developing countries there has been expanded provision of education over the last few decades. Many will charge that in expanding provision, standards have fallen. If a country is attempting to provide schooling for all of its primary and secondary school population, then it is logical to assume that a wide variety of ability levels and background factors will be interacting with teaching and learning, and generally there may well tend to be a high failure rate. How then must we make sense of the charge here that standards have fallen from what they were a few decades ago? It seems safe to say that the sense in which standards have fallen is related to the inadequacy of the system in effectively teaching students with a wide continuum of aptitudes, abilities and background characteristics. There is a general feeling that schools are not as effective as they used to be and that this is reflected in a downward spiral of under-achievement.

The situation also seems to be clouded by value judgements about the way in which education is being transmitted. Many people have definite ideas about what is a sound education and what are important and valuable areas of study. Methodologies that involve student centred learning may seem time-consuming and lacking in rigour, given the demands of the examinations students have to sit. When improvements in curricula and innovative teaching methods do not seem to result in widespread higher achievement, there is a call for 'back to basics'.

This essentially means a concentration on literacy and numeracy, emphasis on drill and repetition and constant testing and monitoring of 'standards'.

The notion of education as a journey into a world of new and exciting experiences, involving the full participation of the student, retreats before a notion of education that is highly circumscribed by what ought to be taught, how it should be taught and 'accountability testing'. When one is trying to ensure accountability in the education system and sees that task as a strict maintenance of standards, the notion that not all standards can be adequately tested by the means we have at our disposal, or, even that 'standards' is an ambiguous concept, is inconvenient. Box 8 below explores at least three different understandings of the term 'standards'.

## Box 8

### 'Learning' and 'Education' Standards

The World Conference on Education for All recognised that people's learning needs are very broad and varied: they 'comprise both essential *learning tools* (such as literacy, oral expression, numeracy and problem solving) and the basic *learning content* (such as knowledge, skills, values and attitudes) required by human beings to be able to survive, to develop their full capacities, to live and work in dignity, to participate fully in development, to improve the quality of their lives, to make informed decisions, and to continue learning' (Article I of the *World Declaration on Education for All*). In light of this, a 'learning standard' may be defined as a specific set of 'learning tools' and/or 'learning content' in the senses indicated above. In principle, it is understood that there exists a procedure for ascertaining whether a person has attained any given learning standard.

An 'education' standard may be defined narrowly as a learning standard that an educational programme aims to help learners attain or more broadly and colloquially as encompassing both the 'learning' standard aimed at and the whole complex of characteristics of the educational programme, for example class sizes, teachers' qualifications, textbooks required, conditions of the physical plant, and so on, associated with the standard. In this broader sense the term 'education standard' is virtually synonymous with 'educational quality'.

It is useful to draw a distinction between a prescribed learning or education standard on the one hand and a standard of performance or attained standard on the other. That they do not always coincide is reflected in the frequency of public complaints of 'falling standards', when the reference can be understood narrowly – depending on the context – to refer to level of learning achievement or performance of students in a particular educational programme or, more broadly both to this fall in learning achievement as well as a deterioration in the material conditions required to implement the educational programme under consideration. In this broader sense 'falling standards' is virtually synonymous with a 'decline' in the 'quality of education'.

*Source:* Adapted from UNESCO, 1993, p. 78

## Activity 7

*Consider these tasks based on the previous and following boxes:*

- *Conduct a small survey of educators and members of the public to determine their notion of 'standards' in education. Do they equate standards with: achieved levels of proficiency as handed down by public examinations? Or is there more of an understanding of standards as a set of prescriptions detailed beforehand that students should attain? Do they subscribe to a broader notion of standards, as in the determinants of educational quality? Or is there some other understanding of 'standards'?*

- *Identify the sense in which the term 'standards' is used in Box 9 below.*

## Box 9

### Average Performance of Students in a Curriculum Area

If the individual scores of a representative sample of students in a country are added and then divided by the number of students, one gets an overall average for performance in a particular curriculum area, at a particular age, for that country. The procedure may not be quite as simple as this in practice, since adjustments may have to be made to take into account the disproportional sampling of students in different regions or types of school. The basic point, however, is that one is seeking to represent in quantitative terms the average level of performance in the country.

This information is of limited value in itself because it does not tell us whether the average obtained can be regarded as 'satisfactory' or 'unsatisfactory'. It can be useful, however, if comparative data are available with which the obtained average score can be compared. Thus, the information could be useful as an indication of whether standards in the country were, in general, stable, rising, or falling, if comparable information were available from an earlier point in time. It could also be useful if similar information were available from other countries, as is the case in international studies of assessment.

*Source:* Adapted from Greaney and Kellaghan, 1996, p. 63

## Summary

Putting this together, we come up with an understanding that all the senses of the term, 'standards', are related. When developing curricula, educators are mindful of the general prescribed minimum levels of competencies that world organisations and or national development plans lay down as desirable to upgrade the human resources of a country or region. In turn, these competencies guide the decisions of public examination and national assessment bodies in how they create test items, mark and grade scripts. And, certainly these 'minimum competencies' can be better transmitted in classrooms equipped with trained personnel and up-to-date resources. Hence, if persons only identify one 'sense' by which they understand 'standards', it is obvious that that implicitly invokes the other 'senses' with which 'standards' are associated. As an example, refer to Box 10 where there are regional prescriptions of standards, expected to be attained through the specific and general objectives of curricula and examinations. If there is a 'gap' between what has been prescribed and what is attained, then one can reasonably question the 'quality' of education being delivered.

---

**Box 10**

**Defining Educational Standards in the Eastern Caribbean**

Quality education is broadly defined in terms of educational standards expected of students at the end of secondary schooling. They should:

(a) Possess literacy and numeracy skills that allow them to:

(i) read with comprehension newspapers or magazines; health, disaster preparedness or agricultural bulletins; (ii) write legible letters in standard English to a friend, prospective employer or Government bureau; (iii) express views in an articulate and logical manner; (iv) handle important basic computations in everyday financial transactions;

(b) Know how to find information through the use of libraries, directories and encyclopedias, maps and charts, and modern electronic devices;

(c) Demonstrate positive habits and good interpersonal skills in the interaction with family, community, visitors and in group relationships generally;

---

(d) Demonstrate reasonable understanding and appreciation of scientific and technological processes as these pertain to nature, the environment and everyday life;

(e) Demonstrate a working knowledge of and functional capacity in at least one foreign language;

(f) Have an appreciation for a wide range of music, art, dance, dramatic expressions, and have some practical competence in expressing oneself in at least one of these areas;

(g) Possess functional knowledge and skills to facilitate entry into the world of work or to continue formal education;

(h) Possess functional knowledge and skills needed for civic participation –

   (i) as citizens of a democratic state,
   (ii) as participants in civic organisations,
   (iii) as members of the Caribbean Community;

(i) Hold to a value system that espouses a noble vision of Caribbean society and of Caribbean people and high principles pertaining to personal integrity, honesty, truthfulness and goodness.

*Source:* OECS, 1991, pp. 71–72

## Activity 8

*Consider this task and these questions:*

- *Which of these standards are relatively 'easy' to test via traditional curricula and assessment practices?*

- *Research the topic 'Educational Objectives'. Identify the standards above, which lie in the 'affective' domain.*

- *It is possible that some affective objectives can be tested via 'authentic assessment'. Research this topic and evaluate to what extent authentic assessment is used in schools or public and national assessments.*

- *How valid is the proposition then that educators or the public in general can pronounce on 'falling standards?'*

## Prescribed standards in specific curriculum areas

It is only in the specific curriculum area of literacy that there have been extensive international efforts to come up with a common standard of a literate person and translation of this into nationally prescribed standards at every stage and level of schooling.

> *A person is functionally literate who can engage in all those activities in which literacy is required for effective functioning of his [her] group and community and also for enabling him [her] to continue to use reading, writing and calculation for his [her] own and the community's development.* (UNESCO, 1993, p. 79).

Each country can either devise standardised tests to determine to what extent they are achieving this prescription and/or, they can participate in international literacy surveys so that they have a good idea of where they stand compared to other countries against the standard.

Millward, below, objects to the rigorous institution of standardised testing of reading in schools in the United Kingdom. The purpose of such tests is to ensure accountability – that the education system is delivering the minimum standards prescribed. However, the process of reading is multi-dimensional and testing can only touch few aspects. Emphasis on devising, monitoring and evaluating standards can unnecessarily circumscribe education.

---

### Box 11

**Standards and Basics**

Talk of standards implies carefully defined benchmarks which can be used to describe actions and responses as being correct or incorrect. Standards are decentred, they demand consistency over time and they are applied indiscriminately across a population. Progress against a standard is marked in terms of moving closer to the norm or more nearly meeting the criteria. There are elements of the reading process which can be standardised. It is possible, for example, to identify carefully defined benchmarks (dictionary definitions of words or grapho-phonic correspondence) and to record correct and incorrect responses (right answers to comprehension exercises or correct pronunciation). It is possible to treat texts as constant over time ('What is Shakespeare saying here?') and not difficult to set out a hierarchy of features (moving from, say a recognition of initial letters, to vowels, to blends and diagraphs to strings of letters and so on) which describes and prescribes progress.

---

It is possible to describe elements of the reading process in this way, but it is immediately apparent that these benchmarks are not like the standard for measuring railway tracks.

It might be argued that we are only finding our way into describing standard features of the reading process and that, with time and with good teaching, we could expect to refine these benchmarks and make the standards more reliable. The important thing, so it might be said, is that we have identified significant aspects of reading (mostly concerned with decoding skills and the ability to say what a list of words or phrases mean) and that proper teaching of these skills will not only make children into proficient readers but also make the assessment procedures more reliable. After all, it is reassuring to know what to teach and reassuring to know that you have the procedures for deciding whether people have learned their lessons well. It is not hard to see how standardised testing can lead to children being taught the 'basics', and it is more than just a happy world which manages to ensure that the basics in reading are those elements of the reading process which are most easily tested.

However, this approach leads to a sterile account of reading with emphasis upon decoding, word building and 'given' meanings, and it is a description of the reading process which is severely limited. It is also a distortion. That the account represents only parts of the reading process for so long as it is made clear that only aspects of reading are being tested and for so long as there is 'no pretence that the results will tell a teacher or a parent all there is to know about the child as a reader'. However, the data recovered from standardised tests are usually treated as a measure of reading (consider only the implication of giving a child a reading age of, say, 7.9 years) and the standardised elements of the reading process are thereby presented as the essence of reading. That does matter. As readers' performances against these *standards* are seen to fall, it is easy to see how remedial action might be directed towards the *standards*. The 'basics' for success is realising standard performances. It is also easy to see how these *standards* can encourage teachers to take a narrow view of the reading process, a view which is reflected in their teaching and which colours the children's view of what counts as success in reading. This may bring disappointing results, but it helps us to see why the outcomes of reading tests are only rarely unexpected and it points to one of the reasons why the testers are able to claim high levels of content validity for their tests. We are in danger of being knotted up in a closed circle and condemned to a spiral defined by *standards* and 'basics'. Within such a spiral there can be no room for the reading process and it can lead to a curriculum which, 'through the assessment framework emphasises the ability to conform to conventional correctness, and to produce prescribed responses'. The focus is 'almost entirely on a narrow conception of word identification and on children spotting 'correct' meaning in texts. This may be a narrow and dispiriting view of reading, but it lends itself readily to testing.

*Source:* Adapted from Millward, 1994, pp.88–89

---

**Activity 9**

*Consider the following issues:*

- *Should there be one literacy standard for all students at a specific grade level, or several to accommodate individual differences?*

- *Are there other, possibly more meaningful ways, of setting standards? Investigate different approaches to setting standards (Tuijnman et al., 1994).*

- *Identify the ways in which the setting, monitoring and evaluation of standards are a 'values-laden' exercise.*

---

## International evaluation of educational assessment

When a country embarks on national assessments of its education system in the interests of greater accountability, it often has to become involved as well in international comparisons to obtain a more complete picture of what the system is achieving. What exactly will be compared? A score of some kind measured against a standard. National assessments need to be compared to past internal assessments to monitor 'standards' in the country over time, as well as compared to the performance of other countries to determine whether an acceptable level of performance is being achieved at home.

The IEA (International Evaluation of Educational Assessment) has undertaken many cross-national surveys where tests are made as equivalent as possible so that comparisons can be meaningful. The IEA also extends assistance and technical expertise in other ways of assessing the system – the emphasis is not only on testing. We are going to look in some detail at the experience of the Dominican Republic (Box 12) in carrying out assessments of its education system with the help of the IEA. You will notice that both qualitative as well as quantitative data are collected so that the notion of 'standards' that is being invoked here has to do with data derived from tests as well as from qualitative factors having to do with the conditions and context of learning.

---

## Box 12

### Dominican Republic: The Study on Teaching and Learning of Mathematics

Most policy-makers do not know the educational achievement scores in mathematics and language attained by students spending a few years in the classroom. Therefore they do not know if the quality is better or worse over time. Unfortunately, many Latin American countries still lack national evaluation systems to determine curriculum areas that need improvement – systems that can generate innovative and viable programmes to improve instruction and learning in the various curriculum subjects. In fact, it is often left to the teacher alone to determine whether a student should be promoted to the next primary grade. Under this system, how can one be sure whether standards in one school are the same as standards in another?

In 1980, a group of professors initiated the TLMDR (the teaching and learning of mathematics in the Dominican Republic) project. Dominican professors decided to pool their knowledge in different areas to focus on a neglected but important aspect of education – the evaluation of classroom teaching and learning. One reason for interest in classroom mathematics teaching/learning was the perception that educators did not know how well scientific and technological knowledge appropriate to Latin America was being produced in the classroom. The lack of sufficient Dominican Republic college students interested and competent in the sciences could also be traced to poor teaching of basic sciences and mathematics in primary and secondary schools. In fact, educators had very little reliable information concerning the quantity and quality of mathematics learned by students in the Dominican Republic. Moreover, very little was known about the way teachers taught daily mathematics classes.

It was against this background that the IEA International Mathematics Study provided the opportunity to share access to expertise, experience and technological know-how accumulated by the IEA since the late 1960s. National expectations for the study were to receive empirical data which could be used to design new strategies to improve the teaching and learning of mathematics in the Dominican Republic. The strategies would be based on information obtained from national samples of both teachers and students interacting with each other in the instructional framework. Comparisons with other education systems, both similar to and different from the Dominican Republic, could show how well students were doing on the basis of 'the international yardstick'. The earlier study (1980s) paved the way for participation in the newer international mathematics and science study now being conducted in over fifty countries by the IEA.

Like all international comparative studies, TLMDR was conceived as a broad-based, comparative investigation of the mathematics curriculum as prescribed, taught and learned. For the purposes of the study, the mathematics curriculum was seen to consist of three dimensions: intended (official documents), implemented (classroom teaching) and attained (student achievement gain on a pre- and post- test design). In addition to the curriculum analysis, the design allowed the study of several non-school factors, such as family influences, since it is always more appropriate to study an education system within its social context.

TLMDR mathematics tests were administered at the beginning and end of the school year to a random sample of 5,342 students in the target populations (13 and 17 year olds). Achievement tests consisted of a 40-item core and 4 rotated forms of 35 items each, from which students answered the core items and one rotated set of questions. In addition to the mathematics test, a student questionnaire was developed to gather information about parental occupation and education, students' nutritional practices, the occupational expectations of students and attitudes toward school and learning. Similarly, a questionnaire was developed for teachers, requesting information about academic training, teacher workload, instructional materials and practices, opinions about the mathematics process and attitudes towards mathematics. A classroom process questionnaire was developed to gather information about methods and procedures used to teach algebra, geometry, measurement, etc. Finally, a questionnaire was developed which gathered information about the opportunities students had had during their current or previous school year to learn the mathematics needed to answer the test items.

Some findings from the study: all school types in the Dominican Republic were below the international norms, with the private school students performing best among the school types in the country. In fact, the pre-test average score in the private school group was higher than the post-test score in all the other school forms.

*Source:* Adapted from Luna, 1992, pp. 448–51

## Summary

From the above account the following is evident:

- Tests constructed for public examinations cannot be used for the purposes of national assessments although both are created with a similar attention to rigour.

- A national assessment extends far beyond the computation of raw scores and comparison with an international standard.

- National assessments are conceived as multi-faceted exercises where the opportunity is taken to gather as much data as possible on classroom as well as non-classroom factors.

- The notion of standards evident here is the setting of minimum competencies for particular age and grade levels and then comparison across international contexts.

- Low performance measured against the standard should signal that improvements are necessary in the system.

- Given the subjectivity, ambiguity and 'narrow' interpretation associated with the selection, monitoring and evaluation of standards, educators and planners conducting national assessments should be aware that accountability issues cannot be based on quantitative data alone.

- Standards can be regarded as a general indicator of system performance – the host of other contextual data collected indicates awareness that analysis of the system depends on a great variety of factors and standards are just a tool to indicate whether something is wrong.

- National assessments can reveal equity issues entrenched in the system, for example, performance of rural vs. urban schools, private vs. state-owned, denominational vs. non-denominational, or curriculum options that seem aligned to gender, ethnic or socio-economic factors.

- National assessments can also reveal if state funds are being used efficiently. Rapid turnover of teaching staff, high teacher pupil ratios, increasing rates of repetition, attrition and drop-outs as well as a large percentage of students being unable to obtain minimum credentials at the end of secondary schooling signal that investments in education are not realising targeted goals.

- The 'quality' of education is also revealed through the various data collection devices of national assessments. Curriculum analysis becomes a must when large numbers of students are failing to attain minimum standards. Teacher training and classroom strategies also come under scrutiny as well as the calibre of texts and other resources. Teacher opinions are invaluable in pinpointing problems in the system.

## Wrap-up and extended reflection

### Launching a revolution in standards and assessments

The point is that standards will be meaningless if students continue to be tested without regard to them. Unless current tests change, the standards will wither and die. Teachers know that they will be judged by test results, and they will continue to teach to the tests by which they are judged. Tests must test knowledge and skills that are meaningful to students. The tests should be based on what children learn in class, and what they learn in class should be worth knowing and doing and using.

Standards are the starting point of education reform. You cannot design an assessment unless you have agreement about what children should learn. In the absence of national standards, we have evolved a haphazard, accidental, disconnected national curriculum based on mass-market textbooks and standardised, multiple-choice tests.

Education reform must begin with broad agreement on what children should learn. Learning, after all, is the heart and soul of education. When there is no agreement regarding what students should learn, then each part of the education system pursues different, sometimes contradictory, goals. As a result, our education system is riddled with inequity, incoherence, and inefficiency.

In the summer of 1991 the department sponsored a meeting with education ministers from 15 Asian Pacific countries. The subject of the meeting was standards for the 21st century. The United States was one of the few participants that had not established national standards. When we asked the various ministers why their society had set national standards, they all gave the same dual answer: to promote equality of opportunity and to promote high achievement. As they explained it, without explicit standards some schools would set high standards and others would not (and without assessments, no one would know the difference). Moreover, explicit standards enabled students to judge their performance against clear goals, thus raising everyone's expectations.

Ravitch, 1993, p. 772

## Suggested reading

Anderson, S, Ball, S and Murphy, R (1975). *Encyclopedia of Educational Evaluation*. NY: Jossey-Bass.

Greaney, V and Kellaghan, T (1996). *Monitoring the Learning Outcomes of Education Systems*. Washington, DC: The World Bank.

Lockheed, M (1996). 'International Context for Assessments' in P. Murphy *et al.* (eds.) *National Assessments – Testing the System*. Washington, DC: World Bank.

Luna, E (1992). 'Dominican Republic: The study on Teaching and Learning of Mathematics', *Prospects*, XXII (4), pp. 448–54.

Millward, P (1994). 'Making Sense of Standards in Reading', *Evaluation and Research in Education*, 8 (1&2), pp. 85–96.

Murphy, P, Greaney, V, Lockheed, M and Rojas, C (eds.) (1996). *National Assessments – Testing the System*. Washington, DC: World Bank.

Nwama, O C (1996). 'What are national assessments and why do them?' in P. Murphy *et al.*, (eds.) *National Assessments – Testing the System*. Washington, DC: World Bank.

OECS (Organisation of Eastern Caribbean States) (1991). *OECS Education Reform Strategy*. St. Lucia: CIDA.

Ravitch, D (1993). 'Launching a Revolution in Standards and Assessments', *Phi Delta Kappan*, 74 (10), pp. 767–72.

Tuijnman, A and Postlethwaite, T (eds.) (1994). *Monitoring the Standards of Education: Papers in Honour of John P. Keeves*. Oxford: Pergamon.

UNESCO (1993). *World Education Report, 1993*. Paris: UNESCO Publishing.

Wiley, D and Wolfe, R (1992). 'Major Survey Design Issues for the IEA Third International Mathematics and Science Study', *Prospects*, XXII (3), pp. 297–304.

# MODULE 7
# Project planning

## Background

In most development programmes the objectives of the programme become concretised when these programmes are reduced to actual projects. The actual project must reconcile the conflict between ideals and reality; between resources and intentions; between competing needs and wants and between the future and the present.

Much of the greater part of the work of most multilateral and bilateral donors revolves around the project. A project can be defined as a coherently linked envelope of resources designed to fulfill a set of development objectives. Indeed, the project is the main link between the mobilisation and the disbursement of aid funds. In a nutshell the project can be viewed as the vehicle that translates external funds into an objective-driven package of resources that are organised and scheduled in such a way as to meet identified needs. The project has a time limit for the production of intended results, a work plan, a schedule of inputs and a budget. The monitoring and evaluation of a project determines substantive achievements and accountability for the expenditure of technical co-operation resources.

This module on project planning sets out to introduce policy makers to the different stages of the project cycle. The module consists of two sections. Section 1 looks at the stages of the traditional project cycle and introduces the new World Bank Project Cycle. Section 2 introduces the reader to simple techniques of project analysis.

## Objectives

At the end of Section 1, the participant should be able to:

1. Distinguish the different stages of the project cycle;

2. Clarify the tasks to be performed at the different stages;

3. Provide a rationale for each stage of cycle;

4. Identify key concerns and errors which may be made at the different stages;

5. Appreciate the role of different stakeholders in the design and execution of projects;

6. Explain the rationale for the new World Bank project cycle.

## Instruction 1

Read Box 1.

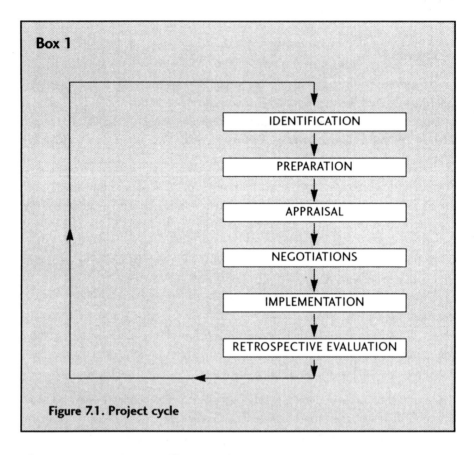

**Box 1**

IDENTIFICATION

PREPARATION

APPRAISAL

NEGOTIATIONS

IMPLEMENTATION

RETROSPECTIVE EVALUATION

**Figure 7.1. Project cycle**

## The successive stages of a project

The life of a project is usually divided into several consecutive stages. This sequence (see Box 1) is often known as the project cycle, because each stage is the logical successor of the preceding one, while the last stage prepares the first of the next cycle.

In practice, the distinctions between the various stages are not always sharply drawn. In some projects, the first two or three stages are more or less merged, and in others there is no retrospective evaluation. On the other hand, projects financed by international aid sources generally follow the cycle quite closely. Despite these variations, it can be stated that the broad outline of the cycle is followed by most education projects. We now briefly review the different stages, examining the purpose, the agents and the process of each. (Magnen, 1991, UNESCO, p. 27)

## Activity 1

1. *Do these different stages seem logical if one had to plan a project?*
2. *Why would lending agencies require that borrowers follow this cycle very closely?*

*Instruction 2*

Read Box 2.

## First stage of project cycle

*Project identification*

### Box 2

The purpose of *identification* is precisely to select one or several projects with high priority for the country's development and then to define their objectives, strategy and main characteristics. This early selection means that the long and expensive stage of preparation can be reserved for those projects whose priority is *justified*. Thus the main function of identification is to *justify* the priority of identified projects. To justify an education project is to show that it has high priority, in that it is likely to substantially improve the performance of education. It is also to show that the project is in conformity with the national development and education policies. The responsibility for identifying education projects usually falls on the Ministry of Education, and in particular the unit entrusted with planning. (Magnen, *op. cit.*, p. 28)

## Activity 2

1. *How can a project identification report help in initial discussions with lending agencies?*
2. *How can a study of the education sector assist in project identification?*
3. *Would consultation of all stakeholders at this stage contribute to the success of a project?*

## Summary

A common problem at this stage is the concentration on the funding necessary and the way funds will be consumed rather than the proper analysis of the problem to be solved. Another common problem is the setting of unrealistic and unachievable goals. Another is the lack of a thorough consultative process.

### Instruction 3

Read Box 3.

### Project preparation

---

#### Box 3

Project *preparation* has two main purposes: studying in detail all the aspects of the project, so as to ensure that it is reasonably feasible; planning its execution, so that it can start without delays. As in the case of identification, responsibility for the preparation of education projects generally falls on the Ministry of Education concerned.

Contrary to identification, project preparation is a long and costly operation. It studies all the aspects (technical, institutional socio-political, economic and financial) that have a bearing on the project's success. It details the necessary investment items, quantifying their costs, as well as the additional recurrent expenditure generated by the project. It envisages the organisation to be provided and the measures to be taken for the project execution, as well as the subsequent functioning of the institutions concerned. Preparation often requires carrying out pre-investment studies, with a view to selecting the most appropriate technical or institutional approaches. All this takes time, but this is far from wasted if the work is well done. Experience has shown, in fact, that detailed preparation is one of the keys to project success, and can result in significant savings on the required outlay. (Magnen, *op. cit.*, p. 29)

---

## Summary

This can be a very lengthy period of the project cycle and can involve considerable expense. Feasibility studies and cost benefit analysis may be done at this stage. Lending agencies may stipulate procedures at this stage. The preparation of a project plan is therefore a fairly complex affair.

The problem has to be properly identified and a proper needs assessment done. This would require a consultative process which can be difficult to manage and coordinate. There is a great temptation for politicians to identify projects, not to satisfy felt and relevant needs, but for political mileage. The required data and personnel for carrying out feasibility studies may not be readily available. In addition, assessing the full range of interventions for the successful implementation of the project takes a lot of time and planning. Omission of necessary dimensions of the plan would entail future revision.

## Project appraisal

The project preparation report and its attachments (pre-investment studies, architect's drawings, call for tender documents) are transmitted to the authorities responsible for financing, and are studied by the competent services before the decision to approve or reject the project is taken.

*Appraisal* is therefore more or less an in-depth study of the project by the government departments or organisations that are to arrange for financing (Ministry of Planning or of Finance, external aid sources) before approval is given.

Like identification and preparation, appraisal has the goal of ensuring that the project is justified and feasible. In addition, it must verify that the project has been sufficiently well prepared for implementation to start as soon as the project has been approved. Coming under the responsibility of financial decision makers, in the appraisal of an education project particular importance is attached to its integration with the overall set of national activities, as well as to its economic and financial aspects.

All projects must be evaluated to determine whether they are suitable and more desirable that other projects.

The criteria for appraisal include:

1. Educational feasibility;
2. Technical feasibility;
3. Financial feasibility;
4. Socio-political feasibility;
5. Administrative feasibility;
6. Institutional feasibility.

Points to consider:

Consider each criteria 1–6 above and state the factors one would consider in each category in order to evaluate a project.

## Project design

Consider these key questions:

1. What is the problem and its causes? How is the problem related to human needs?

2 What conditions are expected if the problems are solved?

3 What alternative solutions to this problem are possible?

4 What are the costs and benefits of each? Who will benefit from each possible solution?

5. What is the best solution? Why is it the best solution?

6. Who are the beneficiaries of this solution?

7. What technical co-operation problems, if any, are embedded in the development problem and the proposed best solution?

8. What conditions or results are expected if the technical co-operation problems are solved? What results would this solution achieve? What would be the objectives of a project to achieve these results?

9. What approaches, defined as the sets of outputs and activities, could achieve the intended solution? Which outputs and activities will best achieve the objectives?

10. What sets of inputs and arrangements are possible?

11. Which is the most appropriate set of inputs and arrangements? Why is this set the most appropriate?

12. What are the risks to the production or the relevance of project outputs? If there are any serious risks, how can they be dealt with or avoided?

13. What financial resources are needed from UNDP and the Governments?

## Common iterations in the project design process

Figure 7.2 gives a summary of the project design phase. It shows the cyclical nature of project design. Advanced steps in the project design phase often lead to revisions of early steps in the process.

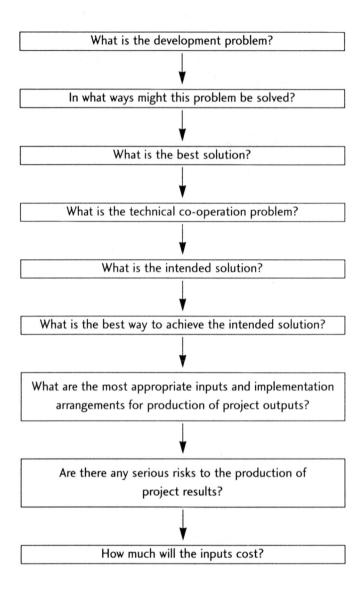

┌─────────────────────────────────────────────┐
│          What is the development problem?          │
└─────────────────────────────────────────────┘
                        ↓
┌─────────────────────────────────────────────┐
│       In what ways might this problem be solved?      │
└─────────────────────────────────────────────┘
                        ↓
┌─────────────────────────────────────────────┐
│             What is the best solution?             │
└─────────────────────────────────────────────┘
                        ↓
┌─────────────────────────────────────────────┐
│     What is the technical co-operation problem?      │
└─────────────────────────────────────────────┘
                        ↓
┌─────────────────────────────────────────────┐
│           What is the intended solution?           │
└─────────────────────────────────────────────┘
                        ↓
┌─────────────────────────────────────────────┐
│  What is the best way to achieve the intended solution?  │
└─────────────────────────────────────────────┘
                        ↓
┌─────────────────────────────────────────────┐
│  What are the most appropriate inputs and implementation  │
│    arrangements for production of project outputs?    │
└─────────────────────────────────────────────┘
                        ↓
┌─────────────────────────────────────────────┐
│      Are there any serious risks to the production of      │
│                project results?                │
└─────────────────────────────────────────────┘
                        ↓
┌─────────────────────────────────────────────┐
│           How much will the inputs cost?           │
└─────────────────────────────────────────────┘

**Figure 7.2. Common iterations in the project design process**

*Instruction 4*

Read Box 5.

**Negotiations**

The appraisal stage usually closes with negotiations between representatives of the Ministry of Education and of the financial decision makers. The negotiations result in an agreement as to the project's objectives, design, content and mode of financing. The Ministry of Education's representatives obviously have a better chance of having their point of view accepted if the project documentation is well prepared, and if they are perfectly familiar with the different aspects. (Magnen, *op. cit.*, p. 30)

**Activity 4**

1. *How would good project identification, preparation and appraisal assist education officials in negotiating with local finance officials and international financial institutions?*

2. *What are the differences in perspectives which the local education official, the local financial official and the International Lending Agency may bring to bear on a project?*

## Implementation

**Box 6**

**Project implementation or management** includes the implementation of all the investments and other actions provided for by the project – construction of buildings, purchase of equipment, training of staff, technical assistance, miscellaneous services, project monitoring and evaluation. It ends when the schools or other institutions developed by the project can function normally. The responsibility for execution of an education project can lie with the Ministry of Education, with another ministry, such as Public Works, or with the donor agency as regards the components of the finances. (Magnen, *op. cit.*, p. 30)

## Activity 5

1. *What factors would determine effective implementation of a project?*

2. *Consider any education project implemented in your country and identify some implementation problems.*

3. *Examine the kinds of institutional arrangements that were necessary for the implementation of any education project in your country.*

**Instruction 5**

Read Box 7.

## Monitoring

### Box 7

Because of the virtually infinite span of thematic and operational activities, the varied target groups, the long term time frame and the qualitative nature of developmental activities in the education sector, monitoring and evaluation processes may be approached from a wide range of perspectives and applied at various substantive, operational and impact levels.

Monitoring may be described as *a continuous process, the continuous nature of which must be entrusted to the periodic and systematic aspect of evaluation.* It relates to the review, analysis and recording of the activities being implemented, with a determination of the level of cost achievements and output relative to programmed objectives, activities, time-frame and expenditure.

*An effective monitoring system should provide for recognition of the positive aspects and the validation of the design and implementation stages and the scope for enhancement of these areas of the project or programme cycle.* Conversely it *serves* as well for identification of the constraints affecting delivery of output. It would also allow *for feedback to the execution mechanism relative to the timely adoption of adjustments and changes in implementation, given that there is the proper design of the system to facilitate this process.*

## Evaluation

## The new World Bank project style

The traditional project cycle – with orderly progression from identification to preparation, appraisal, approval, implementation and evaluation – has been well suited to infrastructural development in stable economies with well established institutions and predictable government policies.

In the present era development business is now more participation, more risky and more volatile. Poor performance on development projects are attributable to: (a) lack of participation by beneficiaries; (b) borrowers not being committed to project goals; (c) inadequate risk assessment; (d) lack of emphasis on capacity building; (e) lack of flexibility. In response, the World Bank has devised a new project cycle.

***Instruction 6***

Study Box 9.

---

**Box 9**

**1. Listening** – In the traditional project cycle, the first step is 'identification' – a term that suggests the visual selection of physical goals. The new project cycle starts with 'listening'. This term symbolises the learning dimension of projects, the central role of the borrower, and the participation of potential beneficiaries right from the start.

**2. Piloting** – The second phase 'piloting' – is geared to exploring alternatives identified at the learning phase and objectively assessing risks. Pilot projects are deliberately small.

**3. Demonstration** – Based on the results of the pilot, the 'demonstration' phase provides the opportunity to fine-tune and adapt project concepts – for example, to confirm hypotheses identified at the pilot phase through trials on a representative scale, and to confirm that risks are manageable and that the project potentially has a satisfactory development impact.

**4. Mainstreaming** – The ultimate aim of development assistance is institutional learning and the achievement of a lasting impact on the country's policies, practices, technologies, and skills. Hence, the new cycle comes to fruition with the large-scale adoption – that is 'mainstreaming' – of methods, techniques, and programmes pioneered during the pilot and demonstration phases.

---

**Activity 8**

1. *How does the new project cycle match up with the traditional project cycle?*

2. *Would the new cycle deal with the shortcomings of the traditional project cycle?*

3. *Is the new cycle friendlier to borrowing countries?*

---

# SECTION 2

## Objective

At the end of Section 2, the participant should be able to:

1. Give a simple explanation of cost-benefit analysis;

2. Explain the concept of net present value;

3. Understand the significance of the discount rate.

## Distinguishing between private cost-benefit analysis and social cost-benefit analysis

**Box 10**

In order to decide whether any project or investment is to be undertaken the investor has to be able to determine how profitable it is compared to other projects. In order to do this a producer will simply determine costs and revenues. If revenues are greater than costs the investment is feasible. If costs are greater then the investment is not feasible. A private produce, for example, a manufacturer of furniture will determine his costs and revenues by his bills and receipts. A state agency building a school may use bills to determine a lot of the costs involved but the revenue side may prove difficult since no actual sales are generated. But there are definite benefits which society enjoys. These are called social benefits. Some investments may incur costs like damage to landscape or pollution and these costs are not borne by the producer. These are called social costs.

**Activity 9**

1. Attempt a cost benefit analysis for the building and equipping of a small primary school in a rural area of your choice.

2. What difficulties do you encounter?

## The concept of present value

### Some considerations in establishing the discount rate

The discount rate is significant since it is the rate used to reduce future streams of profits/benefits to a present value. When market considerations are involved, the rate of interest representing the cost of capital is a useful approximation of the discount rate. The higher the discount rate used the more difficult it is for a project to be approved, i.e. to show a high net present value.

## Suggested reading

Hallat, J (1969). *The Analysis of Educational Costs and Expenditure.* UNESCO.

Lal, D (1974). *Methods of Project Analysis.* Washington, DC: Johns Hopkins University Press.

Magnen, Andre (1991). *Education Projects, Elaboration, Financing and Management.* UNESCO.

Mishan, E J (1976). *Cost-Benefit Analysis.* New York: Praeger Publishers.

Ray, A (1984). *Cost-Benefit Analysis.* Washington, DC: Johns Hopkins University Press.

Squire, L and Van Der Tat, G (1975). *Economic Analysis of Projects.* Washington, DC: Johns Hopkins University Press.

Woodhall, Maureen (1970). *Cost-benefit Analysis in Educational Planning.* UNESCO.

# MODULE 8

## The use of technology

### Overview

Technology is considered today to be an essential tool in everyday living and its impact is increasingly being felt in the realm of education. While many persons – educators and laymen alike – support technological innovation in the curriculum, technology is often viewed as a panacea for the ills of the system. This is largely because of the dizzying pace at which newer and more sophisticated forms of technology have been appearing, each a little more complex and more difficult to understand. Not being able to comprehend each device completely, many people are nevertheless convinced that technology is 'good' for education.

In this module the technology issue, as it applies to education, will be demystified. Basic information will be provided that is relevant to planners in education and finance about the range and possibilities of existing technologies, their relative costs and benefits and the appropriateness of each for different contexts. Also relevant to the topic of educational financing is the potential of technologies, especially the newer technologies, not only to enhance education but to change it.

### Objectives

By the end of this module the participant will be able to:

1. Define technology;

2. Identify the different kinds of technology available to education;

3. Assess the costs and benefits associated with each kind of educational technology;

4. Evaluate the appropriateness of different kinds of educational technologies for different contexts;

5. Recognise the implications of technology in changing traditional notions of education/schooling;

6. Summarise the meanings of the many technical terms associated with 'new' technologies, included in the glossary.

## Introduction

Technology can be simply defined as a tool that can be used to improve the level of performance in any activity. In the case of education, that activity is teaching, with the hope that increased learning will take place.

Technology may appear in the form of printed texts, or technical devices such as overhead projectors. The organised and packaged view of the teaching/learning event into objectives, activities and evaluation using measurement instruments, based on theories which conceptualize learning in terms of inputs and outputs is another aspect of technology in education. Distance education is a technological endeavour because of the considerable know-how necessary to produce and deliver programmes. 'New' technologies refer to computers linked to networks of information.

Planners in Ministries of Education and Finance will need to centre their deliberations on the introduction of technologies into education in terms of improving levels of equity, efficiency and quality in the system. In the context of their situation, they will have to decide which technologies are associated with most benefits relative to costs. On the whole, technology is an expensive innovation so that they must also consider the possibility of partnerships, in paying for desired levels of technology in education. If non-traditional players are being brought into the field of education, then their roles and that of the Ministries of Education and Finance need to be made explicit.

## Equity

Technologies which can enable vast audiences to participate in education, i.e. distance education modes, are often promoted for those countries where universal primary and secondary education have not yet been achieved. However, such technologies have been more evident at the tertiary level to date. They are especially relevant to people hitherto excluded from traditional face-to-face interaction in classrooms, such as those living in isolated areas; those who are disabled in some way; busy, working people; or those who have dropped out of education and would like to continue at their own pace. The potential of distance education technology goes a long way in satisfying the criterion of equity.

## Efficiency

One objective of national governments is to prepare citizens for the world of work through education. Globally, the face of work is changing rapidly and to satisfy the needs of citizens the education system should provide them with the means not only to become technologically literate, but also with the competencies necessary for working in a technology-based environment. This largely refers to the 'new' technologies and satisfies as well the needs of governments because having many citizens technologically educated makes the country well poised to take advantage of opportunities to share in movements towards globalisation and become competitive. If such investments in education pay off in terms of national development, then the system will be considered efficient.

However, the situation differs from country to country. It may be that in some countries planners will have to confine their attention to the provision of basic education, perhaps through distance technologies. Making a sizeable thrust into 'new' technologies in education may not be possible at this time. If the investments in education pay off in terms of providing universal primary education and high graduation rates, then this education system can be considered to be efficient.

## Quality

The development of educational technology is often a collaborative effort between the private sector and education experts. The latter include specialists in writing, editing, subject areas, evaluation, graphics and design, curriculum and educational psychology. Considerable financial outlay is necessary to develop programmes and tools sensitive to learner needs. As a result the technologies help to produce materials of a high standard capable of ensuring learners achieve positive outcomes. This attribute of educational technology can increase the levels of quality in the system.

Once decision makers deliberate on the benefits of equity, efficiency and quality accruing from technological innovation, they then need to consider the cost structures of each kind of technology to assess their cost-benefit ratios. Contextual factors may then help to indicate what technology is appropriate for that particular country.

## Who pays?

Since educational institutions provide the largest market for educational technologies, governments are increasingly entering into partnerships with the corporate sector to intensify the presence of technology in the formal teaching/learning environment. In this way they will be better able to provide for the learning needs of their citizens, and at the same time forge profitable links for business and industry with education while addressing the national development goals of the country.

Increasingly as well, governments are moving away from bearing much of the costs of higher education and allowing those who benefit from education – parents and students – to pay a larger share of what it costs to educate them. Planners need also to bear in mind that the great flexibility of learning brought about by distance and 'new' technologies enables a lot of people to become learners outside of the traditional system. They will pay most of the costs of their own education. It is not a far cry from this to see primary and secondary education being transmitted by non-traditional means, in the long run lifting much of the financial burden from the state.

The expense of technology and its pivotal importance to life today is forcing planners in education and finance to forge links and collaborative structures with many different kinds of organisations that can better facilitate the increased presence of technology in education. This incursion of other groups and interests into education is something that is relatively new to traditional systems. It demands that Ministries of Education and Finance devise a technology plan for education – consisting of broad policy guidelines indicating their preferences for the kinds of technologies to be adopted and their vision of technology in the system as the twenty-first century unfolds. Such a plan will make decision makers focus on what they actually want technology to accomplish and move them to more consistent positions, appropriate for the particular country.

## Issues in the financing of education technologies

What is the range of technologies available to education?

### (i) Classroom-based

The earliest forms of technology in education – the blackboard, chalk and the printed text – are still with us. For most classrooms, especially in countries of the developing world, they continue to be the primary tools of transmission. In North America, Europe and Australia, audio-visual aids have also become commonplace. They include radio and television broadcasts, video presentations, transparencies and overhead projectors, and slides.

These technologies are used by the classroom teacher to better facilitate delivery of educational programmes. They provide interesting stimuli for learners who tend to be more motivated when a variety of resources are used. Learning styles differ and, as a result, better outcomes are ensured by teaching through multi-media technology. Over the last few decades, however, schools from the primary through to the tertiary level in industrialised countries have witnessed the large-scale installation of computers in classrooms. They are typically used as tools in drill and practice, in spelling and arithmetic, in solving equations, in developing graphic skills and to become familiar and adept with 'new' technologies, i.e. accessing the many paths to knowledge open to students who become technologically literate. However, computer use in schools tends to remain orchestrated and controlled by the classroom teacher.

In classrooms throughout Asia, Africa, Latin America and small island states, the provision and use of audio-visual aids are uneven or non-existent. The richer countries and better-endowed schools may have some or all of these technologies, including computers. However, the main concern in developing countries tends to be not the dearth of technology in classrooms, but the dearth of schools. Involvement of technology in education in many parts of the developing world may focus more on accessing previously unreachable populations than on upgrading the quality of transmission in traditional classrooms.

### (ii) Educating at a distance

Distance education refers to a mode of delivering a course of study in which the majority of communication between teachers and students occurs non-contiguously, and the two-way communication between teachers and students necessary for the education process is technologically mediated. (Maxwell, 1995, p. 43)

The earliest form of distance education is more than a century old – the familiar correspondence course – transmitted largely through print materials. Today there is a vast array of different media and combinations of media used in the delivery of distance education – a checklist is given in Box 1. The case of the University of the West Indies is highlighted in Box 2, where distance education is based on the old correspondence course idea of print materials, but with tutorials and video-conferencing built-in. Box 3 describes Mexico's successful venture into providing educational television courses combined with print materials and community-based teachers at the secondary level .

While reading and reflecting on the materials in Boxes 1, 2 and 3, consider the following questions:

- How familiar, as a planner in education or finance, are you with the array of technologies listed in Box 1?

- To what extent do you consider that a sound understanding of these technologies enables you to do your job better?

- Is there a reliance on information from product developers for technological innovation in the education system?

- What is the context of planning in your ministry – is there a clear-cut policy on technology in education?

- Select a technological innovation in education in the recent past in your country. Consider the rationale for choosing the specific mode – were the arguments based primarily on equity, efficiency or quality factors? Who paid and who benefitted?

---

**Box 1**

**List of Distance Delivery Systems**

| Systems | Media | Delivery mode |
| --- | --- | --- |
| Print | Print materials – programmed instruction guided lessons. | Mail |
| Audio | Audio cassette | Mail |
| | Radio broadcast | Radio transmission |
| | Audio teleconferencing | Operator-assisted |
| Electronic graphics | Electronic board | Telephone lines |
| | Fax | Telephone lines |
| Video | Instructional Television Fixed Service (ITFS) | Microwave |
| | Interactive TV; Video Conferencing | Microwave; Cable; T-1 Line; T-3 Line; Fibre Optics; Satellite |
| | Video Tape | Mail |
| | Videodisc | Mail |
| Computer | Computer-assisted instruction | Mail |
| | E-mail Conferencing | Telephone line; T-1 Line; T-3 Line; Fibre optics |
| | Internet; WWW; Digital video conferencing | Telephone Lines; T-1 Line; T-3 Line; Fibre optics |

*Source:* Chen, 1997, p.35

---

Some of the terms used above refer to complex and specialised forms of technology. As an aid to understanding, a glossary has been compiled and is to be found at the end of the module. It will also include other specialist terms used in the module to help the reader clarify his or her understanding of the topic.

---

**Activity 1**

*As an initial exercise before studying how to cost different forms of technology:*

- *Suggest which of the technologies listed above might be cheapest when implementing distance education;*

- *Describe the factors that would cause a country to choose other modes, besides the cheapest, in implementing distance education programmes.*

---

**Box 2**

**Print-driven Distance Education Courses**

The University of the West Indies has begun the process of becoming a dual mode institution, i.e. courses will be offered both face-to-face on the various campuses as well as by distance. Campuses are located in Barbados (Cave Hill), Trinidad (St. Augustine) and Jamaica (Mona). The thrust in distance education is mainly aimed at learners in the non-campus territories, although many other types of learners will find the distance mode convenient.

Courses are to be conveyed largely by print materials specially produced by course development teams. The print materials consist of a Study Guide which contains the course content and assignments and a Course Reader consisting of the assigned readings for the course. Each student has the opportunity to meet with the Resident Tutor in his/her home territory for tutorial purposes. Each semester, the Course Tutor from one of the campuses, will give three two-hour teletutorials. These can be both audio and video conferencing and are primarily for raising questions and issues rather than for delivery of content.

In 1995 a needs assessment was conducted to establish the level and types of need for distance education within the English-speaking Caribbean. The study revealed a strong demand for tertiary level courses in all territories, particularly at the certificate and degree level. While

---

most reactions were cautious because the participants were unaccustomed to the distance mode in learning, they said that they would settle for it if some face-to-face contact could be included. Learning at a distance was readily appreciated for the convenience it afforded them in remaining employed while participating in tertiary level courses.

*Source:* Adapted from UWI, 1996

---

## Activity 2

1. *Suggest reasons why the 'old' correspondence course idea is now considered inadequate for the transmission of distance education.*

2. *What do you think are the challenges of developing print-based materials for distance education courses?*

3. *The main thrust of distance education technologies in the West Indies has been at the tertiary level. Consider why that is so, especially when universal secondary education has not yet been achieved.*

4. *How will the philosophy of educational technologies directed at the secondary school learner differ from that developed for learners at the tertiary level?*

---

## Box 3

### Providing Secondary Education through Television – Telescundaria, Mexico

One of the most successful and sustained distance education efforts in the world is Mexico's well-known Telescundaria programme, initiated in 1968. Telescundaria is now an important component of Mexico's educational system, providing access to quality secondary education to 690,000 students throughout rural Mexico through a combination of television programming, books, and community-based teachers. It grows at a rate of almost 20 per cent annually.

Mexico's satellite capability has made possible ready access to students living in rural communities of less than 2,500, where access to conventional secondary education is particularly limited. Telescundaria today serves students in almost 12,000 schools.

In a landmark of international collaboration, Mexico's Ministry of Education, its domestic satellite authority and several Central American nations agreed in 1996 to use Mexico's Solidaridad Satellite for international utilisation of Telescundaria. Costa Rica is the first to implement such plans. Mexico is making available an invaluable store of 3,600 fifteen-minute television programmes and associated texts and teacher guides, which are being supplemented by Costa Rican programming.

Telescundaria is remarkable in its full institutionalisation within Mexico's Ministry of Education, its continued commitment to both growth and quality and the smooth co-ordination between community teaching resources and nationally produced educational programming. Its new regional approach marks a breakthrough. By overcoming traditional resistance to the use of educational materials developed elsewhere and by combining those with local programming, the economies of scale inherent in educational broadcasting can be realised more fully.

*Source:* Adapted from Block, 1998, pp. 149–150

## Activity 3

1. *Refer to Box 1. Is the Telescundaria programme more likely to be ITFS or interactive TV?*

2. *What are the hallmarks of excellent television programmes produced for distance education?*

3. *Suggest what may be the thinking behind the adoption of radio and television in Latin America as its main distance education modes, rather than print-based materials or computer networking technologies.*

4. *Consider the view that distance education technologies try to duplicate the classroom environment of a good teacher.*

5. *Consider also that such technologies occur on a continuum from the 'old' correspondence idea of little interaction to present multi-media systems designed to foster and simulate such interaction.*

6. *Consider the proposition that all distance education modes examined up to now are an attempt to duplicate the classroom-based environment where there is a good teacher.*

7. *Summarise the advantages and disadvantages of distance-based education and classroom-based education.*

However, there are distance-education delivery systems, based on 'new' technologies, which differ in fundamental ways from traditional classroom-based teaching. Such technologies are derived from computers networked to interface with other devices and information systems that are generally called Information Technology. Box 5 describes some aspects of this latest addition to the store of distance delivery systems and Box 6 looks specifically at a major component of information based technologies – the internet.

---

**Box 4**

**Enter Information Technology**

Compact discs and CD-Roms, micro-computer-based laboratories, the Internet, virtual reality, local and wide area networks, instructional software, Macs, PCs, laptops, notebooks, voice mail, e-mail, satellite communication – the list of 'hot' technologies available for education goes on and on. Can these technologies help the education strategist face the challenge of an education for all in an age of globalisation?

*'Information technology is the fundamental underpinning of the science of structural re-engineering. It is the force that revolutionises business, streamlines government and enables instant communications and the exchange of information among people and institutions around the world. But information technology has not made even its barest appearance in most public schools. Before we can get the education revolution rolling, we need to recognise that our public schools are low-tech institutions in a high-tech society. The same changes that have brought cataclysmic change to every face of business can improve the way we teach students and teachers. And it can also improve the efficiency and effectiveness of how we run our schools'.*
(Gerstner, Jr., (1995), speech to the US National Governors' Association)

**Role of Information Technology**

*1. Improvement of learning and instructions*
Technology can be very powerful as an instructional tool for basic skills. It is infinitely patient with drill-and-practice. It can store and retrieve immense databanks of facts, sample problems, exercises and other curriculum resources. These are the areas in which the information management technologies are most valuable – storing, processing and retrieving information.

Technology can also be powerful in driving new approaches to learning that involve more student interaction, more connections among schools,

---

more collaboration among teachers and students, more involvement of teachers as facilitators and more emphasis on the skills of information seeking and assessment, exploration of open questions, problem-solving, critical thinking, design and construction of new knowledge and understandings. A key understanding is that these new approaches are quite different, with different objectives.

### 2. Improvement of policy planning, design and data management

Education policy development is an intricate process that requires reliable and timely data that are policy-oriented and user-friendly. Here information can be valuable in storing and analysing data on education indicators, student assessment, physical and human educational infrastructure, cost and finance. The technology can help not only in diagnosis but, more importantly, it can assist in constructing scenarios around different intended policy options to determine requirements and consequences. Each scenario can then be systematically analysed and evaluated, not only in terms of its educational desirability but also in terms of financial affordability, feasibility and sustainability over a sufficient period of time to show results.

### 3. Support of educational personnel

Technology allows teachers to overcome the isolation they experience in their schools and provides them with continuous professional development. Connected to an information infrastructure, teachers can communicate with other teachers and professionals and can access data banks, libraries and other vast stores of information. As technology in the school allows teachers to perform traditional tasks with a speed and quality that were unattainable before, it will permit better use of their time not only to teach differently but also to develop professionally.

### 4. Improvement of school management

The same elements of computing and telecommunications equipment and service that made businesses more efficient and cost-effective can be applied to schools and school systems to enable principals and superintendents to streamline operations, monitor performance and improve utilisation of physical and human resources. Technology also has the potential to support the management of complex, standards-related instructional processes in ways that have previously been achieved by only the most advanced schools and skilled teachers. It can also promote communication among schools, parents, central decision makers and businesses, fostering greater accountability, public support and connectivity with the marketplace.

*Source:* Adapted from Haddad, 1998, pp. 23–27

The view expressed above is that Information Technology is the inevitable tool for organising and facilitating all aspects of life in the twenty-first century. Its advantages for education not only encompass new and flexible ways of learning at a distance, but also seem invaluable to policy makers in ministries, as well as to teachers and principals in their different pursuits. Given all these uses, what role can policy makers give to Information Technology when they are devising educational strategies for small states?

## Box 5

### How are Networks Used for Education?

The concept of 'Internet' refers to a vast network of interconnected computer networks that enables computers of all platforms to share services and communicate directly. The Internet refers to the public network, while intranets are *private* networks, with gateways to the Internet accessible only by members of that organisation. The Internet is a progeny of the first computer network in the world, the ARPANET, which was inspired by the need to share resources, to facilitate human communication and interaction, and to augment human intellect through distributed collaboration. This vision is being fulfilled by educational applications of networking.

The ARPANET began in 1969, and electronic mail over distributed networks was invented in 1971. Educational applications of computer networks followed almost immediately. By the mid-1970s, academics began to use computer networks to augment educational activities in their university classrooms and network learning began.

An overview of on-line education and training indicates that the Internet and intranets can be employed in one of 3 modes: adjunct mode, mixed mode and totally on-line mode. In *adjunct mode*, networks are used to enhance regular classrooms and distance education. The major applications involve enriching classroom activities by using networks for class discussions; extending office hours for Q&A; assignment submissions; enabling class collaboration and team projects; enhancing group knowledge, work, and analysis; and expanding access to communities of learners, practitioners, experts, and research resources. Networked classroom approaches (linking classes in different disciplines and/or countries), TeleApprenticeship, Ask an Expert and Electronic Field Trips are examples of adjunct mode applications. In *mixed mode*, a significant portion of the educational activity occurs on-line, while the remainder occurs in traditional mode of face-to-face classrooms or distance education. The applications include professional development programmes, continuing education, training, credit courses, and labs. In *totally on-line mode*, all education or training activity is conducted on-line. Examples include on-line courses special interest courses,and just-in-time training.

*Source:* Adapted from Harasim, 1998, pp. 184–85

## Summary

This section of the module has explored the range of technologies available to education – both classroom-based and at a distance. The next section will deal in detail with costs.

The issues raised in this section concerned:

- the potential of technology to raise the levels of equity, efficiency and quality in the education system;

- the need for decision makers to become more knowledgeable about the various options in educational technology and to have at least a general understanding of the specialist terms associated with 'new technologies';

- factors relevant to the choice of appropriate technology for a country or region, for example contextual considerations such as whether basic literacy has already been established or whether print or television is a better medium given the intended audience;

- an understanding of the bulk of distance education technologies as striving to duplicate the learning environment of classrooms – the more effective distance education programmes involved a mix of media more likely to simulate face-to-face interaction;

- the potential of 'new' technologies

  - to transform education by providing learners with a means of becoming independent of formal, directed structures (either classrooms or conventional distance education media)

  - to be applicable not only to learners but also to teachers, principals and policy makers as a training and information management tool

  - in facilitating the transition of developing countries towards values and practices more clearly aligned to the global information economy

– as a problem within the context of small, developing states;

- the increasing involvement of partners (business and industry as well as loan agencies) in the provision of educational technology, resulting in a reduction of costs to the government;

- the need to establish a technology plan for education at the policy level.

This section has explored the range of technologies available to education – both classroom-based and distance-based. The next section will deal in detail with costs.

## The costing of educational technologies

### Why cost?

The array of educational technologies has the power to beguile. Notwithstanding this apparent allure, planners must engage in a rigorous cost analysis of the proposed intervention. This is imperative not only because of scarce resources, but because citizens entrust their monies to public officials to be spent wisely and responsibly. For example, there must be caution in imitating the experience of developed countries where the costs of technology are lower and so the cost per pupil, in terms of average per capita income, is less of a burden to the population than it is in developing countries.

Lessons abound as well in the many technological innovations that have turned out to be white elephants. Take the case of Trinidad and Tobago. In the 1970s and 1980s large revenues were earned in the petroleum sector. Human capital theory urged educational investment in citizens as being the primary resource in fostering national development. This thinking drove a massive school building programme, of junior secondary schools and senior comprehensives, complete with an extensive array of curriculum choices from academic and pre-technician to industrial arts. The emphasis was on provision and access, rather than quality and efficiency. Today, these schools continue to be plagued by an image problem – spectacular and chronic failure – and an obsolete technical-vocational specialist curriculum for which much of the equipment lies unused or has broken down. The huge recurrent costs could not be sustained once oil prices fell.

Most of the recent technologies have been produced in the developed world. As third world peoples, we need to be able to separate the hype of the product developers from the utilitarian things we want to know about the product and what it takes to have the product work optimally. Cost is a major factor – 'upfront costs', 'hidden' costs, 'running' costs, unit costs. Engaging in a cost analysis will clearly demonstrate the likely options.

The unit cost that is most often used in analysing the economics of technological innovation, particularly of distance technologies, is the average cost per student. This is more relevant for our purposes than other unit costs, such as the average total cost per graduate or the average cost per teacher, because what makes good economic sense in supplying distance education is the volume of students it serves.

## Not only about costs

Costs by themselves are not a useful tool for analysis, even cost per student. Costs must be kept in perspective, i.e. they must be related to the goals of the education system. To be of value they must be aligned to pedagogical criteria conducive to improving the outcomes of the system. In other words, if costs differ substantially between two modes of technology, planners do not necessarily have to opt for the cheaper medium, but must also consider the capability of each in achieving a range of higher order learning skills. Hence, planners in both Ministries of Education and Finance need to have some in-depth understanding of the pedagogical potential of competing technologies as well as of their relative costs.

## Technology and traditional schooling

A critical view of the whole question of technology in the curriculum, especially in small states where the resources may be particularly difficult to come by, is that they cannot afford *not* to get involved. The traditional way of 'doing' schooling demands a heavy reliance on labour intensive technologies, considered to be much too expensive to be sustained even in the short term.

Teachers in such environments remain central to learning, and small countries continue to have to pay out huge sums as recurrent expenditure in salaries and benefits. When they speak of improving the system, it is envisaged largely in terms of reducing teacher-pupil ratios, training teachers and upgrading their salaries and conditions of work – all expensive options. If this vision of education remains unchanged, such states will find themselves in a spiral of escalating costs without much improvement in quality. Investing in educational technologies, particularly distance technology, based on rigorous cost analysis, becomes a realistic and inevitable economic decision.

## Fixed and variable costs

Fixed costs refer to the investments that must be made initially to make an innovation a reality. In the case of educational technology, this could be the purchase and/or building of the necessary infrastructure. Where computers are being introduced, the fixed costs refer to the purchase of hardware, the writing of software packages, the installation of peripherals, namely printers and scanners, as well as the wiring and surge protectors that may be necessary to safeguard a reliable electricity supply. It also refers to the costs inherent in developing radio and television programmes, and the writing of books or other print materials. If the technology is to make a significant impact on the system, often training has to be instituted and a central mangement capacity maintained. For example, if a country decides that schools must be equipped with televisions and video recorders, personnel have to be trained to maintain and operate this equipment and a central organising body has to be put in place to co-ordinate the management of this operation.

Fixed costs, then, refer generally to the heavy initial investments made to put the form of educational technology in place in the first instance. It is considered 'fixed' because its component costs are not expected to escalate if its users increase. For example, investments in educational television often incur high fixed costs in terms of establishing a broadcast capacity, in user costs of satellites, and payments to producers and those developing the actual programmes. If 10 students or 5000 students are added to the audience, it would hardly affect the fixed costs.

Variable costs are those costs that tend to vary with additional users. In producing distance-education print materials, the fixed costs are those of the course development team, namely writers, editors, graphic artists and word processing personnel. The variable costs are those incurred in distributing materials to additional students and will vary from year to year. If more students enrol, more materials will have to be printed; if face-to-face tutorials are part of the programme, more will have to be scheduled, incurring costs for teacher time; if teletutorials are structured into the transmission of the course and more students come on stream, more centres will have to be built, as may be the case in outlying islands.

Costs can be precisely worked out (Box 6) and compared with each kind of technology, for example classroom-based as opposed to distance technologies (Box 7). It is also possible to compare the fixed and variable costs for each kind of distance technology (Box 8).

## Box 6

### The Basic Cost Function

The total costs of an enterprise are made up of both fixed and variable costs. Fixed costs do not vary continuously in relation to changes in volume of activities, although they may change if activities are ended or if there are very significant changes in volumes. Variable costs tend to increase or decrease directly with fluctuations in the volume of activity.

The basic cost function for any educational system is:

$$T = S^1/_2 + C\ddot{a} + P^1 + F$$

where

T = total cost

S = the number of students

C = the courses which are being developed

P = the number of courses being presented to students

F = the fixed cost of the system (includes administrative costs and overheads)

$^1/_2$ = the direct cost per student

ä = the direct cost of developing a course

$^1$ = the direct course-related cost of presenting a course

The total direct cost of teaching students is $S^1/_2$, the total direct cost of courses in development is Cä, and the total direct cost of courses in presentation is $P^1$. The variables for which volumes of activity are identified here as being of significance are S, C and P.

*Source:* Adapted from Rumble, 1988, p. 91

## Activity 4

- *In distance education courses, enumerate at least four examples of student-related costs?*

- *Suggest at least four examples of the direct course-related costs of presenting a course.*

- *Which of the factors listed in Box 6 affect variable costs?*

**Box 7**

**Costs and Classroom-based Technologies**

*Blackboards and chalk*

What are their essential characteristics? They are cheap, readily available, portable, require nothing from the surrounding environment to function, need almost no maintenance, and can be mastered by anyone who possesses basic literacy. And they are effective in helping children learn at all educational levels – primary, secondary, and post-secondary. That's pretty good. These are the qualities we might expect the ideal educational technology to have. Blackboards and chalk in fact constitute a kind of benchmark. They help us see what questions to ask when assessing educational technologies. And it seems fair to ask how many of those new technologies possess all – or even a few – of the qualities possessed by blackboards and chalk.

*Source:* Adapted from Puryear, 1998, p. 42

*Teachers*

In conventional teaching, the time of teachers remains the most important element of the costs. In most cases, it accounts for more than half of total costs. In contrast, the fixed costs tend to be modest: the use of the building and equipment and the relatively rudimentary preparation of teaching materials. Under those conditions, there are no significant returns to scale. As long as there are enough students to fill one class, it matters little whether they number a dozen or a million.

*Source:* Adapted from Castro, 1998, p. 32

Box 7 suggests that not only is chalk and blackboard cheap and versatile, but it is also effective in teaching at all levels.

**Activity 5**

1. *Do you think students and teachers would agree? When decisions about technology in the classroom are to be made, how much of an input do those at the chalkface have? Are decisions based only on costs and benefits as compiled by supervisors and experts?*

2. *Consider that for conventional classrooms with minimal technologies to deliver quality education, there must be a highly trained, qualified and motivated teaching force – expensive to achieve and maintain (large variable costs). Is this a viable proposition for classrooms in the third world?*

3. *Technologies cater to different learning styles and intelligences and the materials are usually of a high quality. They are also expensive – high fixed costs. Is it feasible to increase the presence of technology in classrooms in the third world?*

4. *Discuss whether conventional classroom teaching continues to be viable in the third world.*

---

## Box 8

### Costs and Distance Technologies

With technology-intensive teaching, the fixed costs predominate and the variable costs are much lower. First of all, the machines must be purchased. Computers cost at least three thousand dollars if peripherals, rewiring and other technical costs are included. TV sets and VCRs and parabolic antennas cost less than that, but still are far more expensive than any other piece of equipment used in traditional classrooms. When we consider the infrastructure necessary for broadcast transmissions of TV signals, the numbers are not at all modest. Satellite reception requires additional equipment that remains expensive despite price drops. By the same token, software for computers and teaching materials for TV programmes are very expensive when they are good.

Variable costs, however, tend to be quite modest with technology-intensive teaching. The main component is instructors or other forms of labour. The variable costs relate to the conventional end of new instructions – namely, the teachers and aides who use them.

The implications of this distribution of costs could not be clearer. The use of new technologies is associated with powerful economies of scale. As noted, under conventional teacher-intensive technologies per capita costs tend to remain the same or almost the same whether there are one hundred or one million students. In contrast, with new technologies, cost depends on how many share the fixed costs of preparation and installation of equipment. A T.V. programme such as Telecurso 2,000,* which cost close to $50 million to develop, will have a cost per student of $5,000 if 1,000 students attend and $10 if 5 million students attend. The latter figure is not an unreasonable prediction for this programme during its lifetime. Educational software which typically may cost $300,000 to produce is usually sold at $20 or $30, due to the huge scale of sales.

Therefore, it is the expected scale of utilisation which should determine the mode of instruction. With few students, one hires a teacher; with thousands of students, technology-intensive alternatives may be less expensive. It is assumed that for every hour of classroom contact, a teacher has to invest another hour of preparation. For every hour of class, it takes five hours to prepare written materials. But every hour of instruction using an interactive CD Rom requires at least 300 hours of preparation. Hence, in order to justify the use of more complex instructional technologies, it is necessary to have a much broader clientele.

*Source:* Adapted from Castro, 1998, pp. 32–33

*Telecurso 2000 is a distance education programme transmitted via TV and video cassettes in Brazil. It offers a basic curriculum to millions of young adult workers, plagued by illiteracy and incomplete schooling. Learning can be individual or as a group in a tele-classroom with an instructor or as informal mentoring in a learning facility equipped with TVs and VCRs. (Falcão, 1998)

## Checklist of costs for educational technologies

### 1. School- or classroom-based:

| Technology | Fixed costs | Variable costs | Recurrent costs |
|---|---|---|---|
| Audio | Purchase of radios/tape recorders, cassettes; production of radio programmes; electrical capacity/batteries | Almost nil. If student numbers rise, more radios can be purchased relatively cheaply | Electricity/batteries; audio cassettes |
| Visual | (i) Purchase of slide and/or film strip projectors; films/slides; screens; an electrical capacity<br><br>(ii) Purchase of overhead projectors; transparencies; markers; screens; electrical capacity | Almost nil. Only one of each kind of projector in an A-V room may satisfy demand – on a rotating class basis An additional OHP wheeled to classes may be desirable | Expanding stock of films/slides; transparencies; markers; electricity; equipment maintenance |
| Audio-visual | Purchase of TV sets, VCRs and video cassettes; production of the programmes; an electrical capacity | Almost nil. One TV and VCR in an A-V room will satisfy demand, on a rotating basis, even if numbers increase | Expanding stock of videocassettes; electricity; equipment maintenance |

| Technology | Fixed costs | Variable costs | Recurrent costs |
|---|---|---|---|
| *Computers*<br>(i) CAI –<br>computer<br>aided<br>instruction | (i) Purchase of<br>hardware – monitors,<br>CPUs, diskettes,<br>scanners, printers;<br>and, software –<br>sometimes multiple<br>copies of the same<br>programme. Paper.<br>Ink cartridges. An<br>electrical capacity,<br>surge protectors. A<br>maintenance contract | More students mean<br>more CPUs, monitors,<br>diskettes, paper,<br>ink, software<br><br>Two-thirds students<br>to one computer is<br>workable, but a 1:1<br>ratio is desirable | Upgrades of software<br>and/or memory capacity.<br>Printing cartridges.<br>Paper. Electricity.<br><br>Renewal of equipment<br>maintenance contracts |
| (ii) Multi-<br>media<br>application | (ii) All the above<br>costs plus hardware –<br>CD-ROMs and a multi-<br>media kit i.e. speakers,<br>headphones, multi-<br>media software, CDs | Additional multi-<br>media kits. Networking<br>capability and client-<br>server configurations | All the above |
| (iii) Computers<br>and Internet<br>access | (iii) All the above<br>plus the installation<br>of several telephone<br>lines, server access<br>charges and modems | It is impractical for<br>a whole class to be on<br>the Internet at the<br>same time, hence only<br>2–4 telephone lines<br>may be installed | All the above plus<br>monthly server access<br>and telephone charges |

## 2. Distance technologies:

| Technology | Fixed costs | Variable costs | Recurrent costs |
|---|---|---|---|
| *Print<br>materials*<br>(i) Corres-<br>pondence<br>courses | Payments to experts<br>for course development;<br>Printing and distributing<br>costs; a central<br>management body.<br>Possibly the cheapest<br>option – must print<br>large volumes to be<br>cost-effective | Costs of printing<br>and distributing;<br>wage bill of tutors<br>and examiners will<br>rise if numbers rise | Updates of courses<br>(possibly once every<br>5/6 years); printing,<br>distribution costs; paper;<br>wage bill; warehousing |
| (ii) Print<br>material<br>with audio<br>video<br>cassettes | Costs as above plus:<br>an electrical capacity;<br>the production of audio<br>and video programmes;<br>the purchase of<br>cassettes to give<br>or lend to students<br><br>More costly than (i)<br>but more interesting<br>materials | Costs as above –<br>reproducing and<br>distributing the<br>materials and<br>payments to tutors<br>will rise if numbers<br>rise | Costs as above. Electricity.<br>If students borrow<br>cassettes there will be<br>administrative costs in<br>tracking and storing<br>the items; if they are<br>given to, or bought by,<br>students there are<br>replacement costs |

| Technology | Fixed costs | Variable costs | Recurrent costs |
| --- | --- | --- | --- |
| (iii) Print material with face-to-face and tele-tutorials (audio/video conferencing) | As in (i) above – course development; printing and distribution; and administrative costs plus an electrical capacity; establishing buildings/learning centres; purchase and installation of transmission equipment; developing a satellite or terrestrial broadcasting capacity; a telephone bridge to connect many sites; conveners – high quality speakerphones; and maintenance contracts [Expensive – high fixed costs but high quality interaction between students and tutors is possible] | If student numbers rise there will be increased costs for: reproduction and distribution of materials and payments to tutors. Also increased building capacity may be needed\n\nExpensive – high variable costs because as student numbers grow so too do the numbers of tutors or the numbers of hours they have to work. Tutor time is expensive | Updates; stock, printing and distribution, wage bill; maintenance of buildings and equipment; telephone line and electricity charges |
| *Radio* Interactive radio broadcasts | Course development costs – both the radio programme and print materials used in conjunction with the broadcasts. A radio broadcast capacity or purchase of airtime\n\n[Radio airtime is relatively cheap. Print materials are to be used during and after the daily broadcasts. Radios are regarded as being ubiquitious – not a cost to the educational authority. A low-cost medium to reach large populations at distance] | Almost nil. This medium tends to be used widely in schools and thus tutor salaries/buildings/infrastructure are already accounted for.\n\nIf numbers increase, costs will be printing and distribution of materials.\n\nIf used for adult learners and remote students, free community centres and local volunteers as tutors can be used | Updates. Electricity charges/batteries. Costs will depend on whether airtime is purchased from a commercial provider or whether the educational authority sets up its own broadcast capacity. If the former, then costs will be mainly airtime. If the latter – maintenance of transmission and studio equipment and the salary bill of broadcast workers |

| Technology | Fixed costs | Variable costs | Recurrent costs |
|---|---|---|---|
| *Television* Interactive television broadcasts | Course development costs for the TV programmes and accompanying print materials Costs for printing and distributing materials. Purchase of TV sets for those who have to use a learning centre. An electrical capacity. Purchase of airtime or costs in establishing satellite links and transmission of programmes. Maintenance contracts | Almost nil. As above<br><br>Although television airtime is expensive, programmes can be beamed at non-peak hours. An education TV channel could be established. For adult learners, courses can be taped via VCRs and played back later | Updates. Printing and distribution of materials. Electricity. Maintenance of buildings and equipment. Satellite/cable or airtime transmission charges. Salary bill for tutors in the field and ancillary workers |
| *Tele-communications Computers* (i) Internet and the World Wide Web | Website construction, on-line course development costs. Hardware : computers and peripherals (for example modems) and telephone lines. Server access charges. Buildings/study centres | If users increase more telephone lines will have to be installed | Monthly electricity, server access and telephone charges. Maintenance of buildings and equipment |
| (ii) E- mail conferencing | Computer infrastructure, modems, telephone lines, server access, buildings | As above | As above |
| *Audio Conferencing* | Telephone system from point to multi-point. Increased line capacity, telephone bridge system and conveners. Buildings/ study centres. Infrastructure | Almost nil tutor costs. One telephone line can transmit to many learners at one site | Long distance telephone charges. Wage bill. Electricity. Maintenance of buildings and equipment |
| *Video Conferencing* (i) satellite | Video production facilities; an uplink to a transponder; satellite dish to receive signals from transponder (the downlink). Buildings/ study centres. Infrastructure | Tutor costs. Building capacity. Usually is one-way video and two-way audio via telephone because of the expense of transponder time | Wage bill. Electricity. Telephone charges. Transponder time US$ 200–800/hr). Maintenance of buildings and equipment |

| Technology | Fixed costs | Variable costs | Recurrent costs |
|---|---|---|---|
| (ii) cable | Cable company charges for airtime. Video production facilities. Certain times are cheap. Students could video-tape sessions and replay later | Almost nil tutor costs. Feed-back via telephone costs. Feed-back via telephone, e-mail, usually not to the cost of the educational institution | Transmission costs, wage bill, maintenance of buildings and equipment |
| (iii) compressed video i.e. two-way audio and visual communication | Video production facilities. Digital technology – T1 or ISDN telephone lines. A codec to transmit and receive compressed signals. An Inverse Mux to allow greater bandwith. Buildings/ study centres | Tutor costs. Building capacity. Very expensive – can supplement other forms of distance education, e.g. to provide feedback | Telephone line charges. Other transmission costs. Maintenance of buildings and equipment. Wage bill |

## Summary

The first section of this module explored the range of technologies available to education. The latter part of the module was devoted to the costs involved in technological innovation in the curriculum. The main issues raised are summarised below:

- the structure of costs for any intervention, namely, fixed, variable and recurrent costs;

- traditional teaching as having minimal fixed costs and high variable costs whereas technology intensive curricula incurred high fixed costs but very low variable costs;

- the cost-effectiveness potential of technological innovation for large populations not yet having achieved universal primary and secondary education, and for tertiary learners who find it inconvenient to be full-time students;

- not only costs are important, but the pedagogical value of the technology. Planners have to ask themselves if the introduction of any technology will significantly improve learning outcomes;

- the learning outcomes appropriate for the context will influence the choice of technology:

  - distance education technologies via the mass media seem to have had phenomenal success in Latin America where the desired outcomes relate to basic literacy and numeracy and citizenship skills;

- tertiary education innovations using distance technologies seem to be successful using print materials as a base where the desired learning outcomes depend on an already literate population;

- the infusion of more interaction between student and tutor, reminiscent of a traditional classroom:

  - learners, even in this highly technological age, still learn best in social situations, for example coming together at a learning centre from time to time to interact with the tutor and other students, or, simulation of such experiences;

  - the 'mix' of technologies promotes interaction. For example, print materials could be delivered with interactive audio and video-conferencing or cassettes; or television and radio broadcasts could be supplemented with print materials;

- the cost factor of developing highly interactive courses:

  - such courses cater to the needs of distant learners and incur high variable costs in terms of tutor time;

  - the less interactive the materials the cheaper they are to produce but the less interesting they are to the learner – and hence of less pedagogical value;

  - older, literate learners may be successful with print-based materials and minimum interaction with the tutor, while younger learners and adults who have not completed their education, may be more motivated using audio and video technologies and accessing tutor help at a study centre;

- the issue of change, namely that traditional teacher costs are high and so, in a context of scarce resources, there is the likelihood of increased investment in distance technologies, but this will ultimately transform the face of education as it has been known:

  - there may be a reluctance on the part of planners to factor in to their technology plans innovations that will be at odds with traditional perceptions of the institution of education;

  - there is the danger that education by distance, offered as an alternative to face-to-face teaching, will be perceived as inferior and that the innovation may flounder on this perception;

- this situation may be less evident in large developing countries where the problem of access has in the past denied education to many;

- it may be more likely in small states where education has been accessible in the past but where today variable and recurrent costs are found to be increasingly prohibitive;

• the extraordinary potential of 'new' technologies to change the way children learn and at the same time prepare them to function in a technology-based society;

• the dilemma posed to developing countries with an obvious and urgent need to become more technologically literate, but plagued by large numbers of functionally illiterate citizens;

• the compromise may be to invest in distance technologies to upgrade the capability of all citizens in basic education before there is widespread access to information technologies;

• however, planners must be aware that in such countries a small, modern, urban sector will develop proficiency in the use of information technologies, creating inequities in the modernisation thrust.

## Wrap-up and extended reflection

### *The flawed logic of educational technology*

When we examine the gap between the promises of technology in education and the reality, what we find is a lot of wishful thinking. Advocates of educational technology are almost always optimistic rationalists – people who believe that technology use is the logical way to produce better instruction.

Alas, the world is not rational and logical choices often fare poorly. For example, technology ought to be a good way to reduce inequities between the haves and have-nots. By introducing technology to poor areas (for example, inner cities, developing countries), it should give people in those areas access to the same knowledge and skills as the well-off. This is a logical premise and one that has been put into practice many times. But it almost never works well, because poor areas lack the support or infrastructure necessary to take advantage of the technology or any outcomes that might derive from it. In such a situation, there are probably many more basic aspects (such as a better overall learning environment or more relevant curricula) which would have greater value and impact. Indeed, in many cases, the reasons for poor learning are not instructional and amenable to improvement via technology. Instead, they are socio-cultural, economic, political, or psychological in nature (definitely not rational). We persist in trying to address these problems through the use of technology because it is the logical thing to do. Technology may have a role to play (for example, teleconferences to share ideas, databases to provide information, desktop publishing, etc.), but it is probably not the real solution.

The field and practice of educational technology has been far too insular in nature, and not well connected or integrated with the other factors that affect education. It has focused almost exclusively on instructional variables to the exclusion of all the other organisational, social, political, and personal considerations at play in a given educational setting. We need to apply technology in a much broader context, as part of a solution or strategy that addresses these other dimensions. We need to stop thinking about learning in strictly rational terms, but as a socio-cultural phenomenon subject to various outside influences. Until we can do so, we should probably use technology as little as possible – in fact, the less the better.

Kearsley, 1998, p. 50

# Glossary

| | |
|---|---|
| Audio teleconferencing | Two-way audio communication in real time between one point to possibly, multi-points, using telephone lines |
| Broadcast radio/television | One-way audio/video communication from one point to multi-points |
| Codec | Acronym for coder-decoder; a device that changes analogue audio or video signals into digital format |
| Computer conferencing | Computers networked to communicate text, video and audio data with each other in real time |
| Digital video conferencing | Two-way audio and video communication in real time between one point to possibly multi-points, using compressed digital signals via digital phone lines |
| Digital technology | The conversion of analogue data into digital format reduces the bandwidth needed to transmit audio and video data |
| E-mail conferencing | Two-way asynchronous communication (electronic mail) from one computer to another using the Internet |
| Interactive radio/television | Communication that is not necessarily two-way or synchronous – radio and T.V. programmes (and print materials as well), produced in a learner centred manner, with the use of supplementary print or cassettes, and with communication between learners and tutors |
| Internet | An electronic information superhighway of many computer networks capable of communicating with each other |
| Inverse mux | A device needed in compressed video transmission which can create greater bandwidth for transmission |

| | |
|---|---|
| Microwave | High frequency radio waves, for point-to-point transmission of audio and video signals |
| Modem | A device enabling a computer to transmit information via a telephone line by converting the computer signals to audio tones; in this way computers communicate with each other |
| T-1 line | A digital telephone line, from point-to-point, leased by users, and used at full or fractional bandwidth |
| T-3 line | A digital leased telephone line that is capable of very fast transmission of full screen, motion video data |
| Telecommunications | The use of telephone lines to transmit audio and video data and to establish communication between computers |
| Transponders | The device in communications satellites which receives signals from the ground (the uplink) and transmits it back to Earth (the downlink), users pay for transponder time |
| Videodisc | A disc of pre-recorded video data that is played on a videodisc player connected to a television screen or interfaced with a computer |
| World wide web | An enormous network of information sites linked via the Internet to computers at any place in the world; documents are coded in hypertext format i.e. key words and phrases in the text can allow the user immediate access to related materials |

## Suggested reading

Block, C (1998). 'Mass Media in The Service of Latin American Education' in Claudio de Moura Castro (ed.), *Education in the Information Age*. NY: IADB, pp. 138–55.

Castro, C (1998). 'Education in the Information Age: Promises and Frustrations' in Claudio de Moura Castro (ed.), *Education in the Information Age*. NY: IADB, pp. 29–40.

Chen, L (1997). 'Distance Delivery Systems in Terms of Pedagogical Considerations: A Re-evaluation', *Educational Technology*, 37 (4), pp. 34–37.

Haddad, W D (1998). 'Education For All in the Age of Globalization: The Role of Information Technology' in Claudio de Moura Castro (ed.), *Education in the Information Age*. NY: IADB, pp. 21–28.

Harasim, L M (1998). 'The Internet and Intranets for Education and Training: A Framework for Action' in Claudio de Moura Castro (ed.), *Education in the Information Age*. NY: IADB, pp. 181–201.

Falcão, J (1998). 'Telecurso 2000: Breaking with the Paradigm of Traditional Education' in Claudio de Moura Castro (ed.), *Education in the Information Age*. NY: IADB, pp. 175–80.

Kearsley, G (1998). 'Educational Technology: A Critique', *Educational Technology*, 38 (2), pp. 47–51.

Maxwell, L (1995). 'Integrating Open Learning and Distance Education', *Educational Technology*, 35 (6).

Puryear, J M (1998). 'The Economics of Education Technology', in Claudio de Moura Castro (ed.), *Education in the Information Age*. NY: IADB, pp. 41–47.

Rumble, G (1988). 'The Economics of Mass Distance Education', *Prospects*, XVIII (1), pp. 90–102.

U.W.I. (1996). Distance Education: Update. Paper produced by the Office of the Deputy Dean for Distance Education, Faculty of Education, University of the West Indies, St. Augustine.